LISTENING POWER **3**

Language Focus • Comprehension Focus • Note-Taking Skills • Listening for Pleasure

Tammy LeRoi Gilbert

Bruce Rogers

PEARSON

Listening Power 3

Pearson Education, 10 Bank Street, White Plains, NY 10606

Staff credits: The people who made up the *Listening Power* team, representing editorial, production, design, manufacturing, and marketing are John Brezinsky, Dave Dickey, Nancy Flaggman, Ann France, Amy McCormick, Liza Pleva, Jaimie Scanlon, Loretta Steeves, and Paula Van Ells.

Text composition: TSI Graphics
Text font: 11.5/13 Adobe Caslon
Illustrations: TSI Graphics
Credits: See page 183.

Library of Congress Cataloging-in-Publication Data
Rogers, Bruce
  Listening power. 1: language focus: comprehension focus: listening for pleasure/Bruce Rogers, Dorothy Zemach.
    p. cm.
  ISBN 0-13-611421-0—ISBN 0-13-611425-3—ISBN 0-13-611428-8
  1. English language—Textbooks for foreign speakers. 2. Listening. 3. Reading comprehension.
I. Zemach, Dorothy II. Title.
  PE1128.R63446 2011
  428.3'4–dc22

                                                                        2010043222

ISBN-10: 0-13-611428-8
ISBN-13: 978-0-13-611428-4

PEARSONLONGMAN ON THE **WEB**
Pearsonlongman.com offers online resources for teachers and students. Access our Companion Websites, our online catalog, and our local offices around the world.

Visit us at **pearsonlongman.com.**

Printed in the United States of America
1 2 3 4 5 6 7 8 9 10—V042—15 14 13 12 11 10

Contents

Acknowledgments

Many thanks to the amazing team of writers: David Bohlke, Bruce Rogers, and Dorothy Zemach. My deepest appreciation to Amy McCormick and Jaimie Scanlon for all their hard work and support. Special thanks and much love to Arthur, and to my parents, Dale and Gloria, for everything.
Tammy LeRoi Gilbert

I would like to thank Amy McCormick for her guiding vision for the book and the series; Jaimie Scanlon for her skillful and thorough editing of the manuscript; Loretta Steeves for her work in shaping the project and bringing it to completion; our fellow Listening Power authors David Bohlke and Dorothy Zemach for their feedback, suggestions, and encouragement. I'd also like to thank the entire staff at Pearson Longman for a job well done.
Bruce Rogers

The authors and publisher would also like to extend special thanks to the following teachers around the world who reviewed the *Listening Power* series and provided indispensable feedback.
Abigail Brown, Assistant Professor, TransPacific Hawaii College; Alison Evans, Senior Instructor, University of Oregon; Amy Christensen, Instructor, Central New Mexico Community College; Matthew Fryslie, Instructor, Kainan University; Ian K. Leighton, Instructor, SungKyun Language Institute; Rosa Vasquez, Instructor, John F. Kennedy Institute of Languages.

About the Authors

Tammy LeRoi Gilbert is a materials writer, editor, and curriculum development specialist living in San Francisco, California. For more than twenty-five years, both in the US and Japan, she has taught and designed English language and test preparation courses. She has served as Academic Director at language schools and at the University of California-Berkeley Extension. Tammy has also been the contributing author for a number of texts for English language students and has created online materials for English for Academic Purposes and English language test preparation.

Bruce Rogers has taught language and test preparation courses to English language learners since 1979. He taught at the Economics Institute, University of Colorado, Boulder for twenty-one years. He has also taught in Indonesia, Vietnam, Korea, and the Czech Republic. He is the author of six other textbooks for English language learners and is the past president of Colorado TESOL. He lives and works in Boulder, Colorado, USA.

Introduction to *Listening Power 3*

To the Teacher

Helping students develop strong listening skills is an important part of any language program. Good listening skills are a necessity in the classroom and the workplace, as well as in social interactions. In addition, standard English-language tests, such as TOEFL©, TOEIC©, and IELTS©, also require solid skills in listening. Listening was once considered a passive skill, but research has shown that successful listening requires the listener's active engagement. Listening is also considered by many learners to be the most challenging language skill.

The *Listening Power* series is designed to help learners meet the challenges of listening in English and provide students with the effective listening strategies that they need. It also provides a wealth of practice materials designed to facilitate listening fluency. It is primarily designed for students in Intensive English programs, at universities and community colleges, and in advanced classes in secondary schools. For that reason, it has an academic "edge": Much of the material focuses on academic lectures and university-based discussions. However, the text includes material from inside and outside the academic environment, recognizing that even the most serious academic student will need to be proficient at listening in a variety of environments in order to succeed.

Listening Power 3 has four separate parts, each related to one of four important elements of effective listening. Unlike other listening skills texts, *Listening Power* does not require classes to begin with the first unit and work their way page by page to the end of the text. Teachers and students are encouraged to skip from part to part and unit to unit.

Part 1: Language Focus—The units in this section target specific language skill areas that are often challenging for learners when they listen. These include advanced-level skills such as understanding reduced forms (such as "wouldja" and "doncha"), intonation patterns, and idiomatic expressions. After each **Skill Presentation,** there is a set of practice activities, followed by the **Put It Together** section, which provides consolidated practice with longer, more challenging listenings centered on an interesting topic or theme. Teachers may choose to have students complete Put It Together exercises immediately after completing the skill sections or use them for later review.

Part 2: Comprehension Focus—This part of the text includes two sub-sections. The units in the **Building Skills** section present skills required to comprehend longer conversations and lectures, such as identifying main ideas, supporting ideas and details; making inferences; distinguishing between facts and opinions; and recognizing the organization of lectures. Each Building Skills unit includes integrated practice activities. The **Applying Skills** units offer high-interest, theme-based listening texts and additional practice activities designed to help students put their new skills to practical use.

Part 3: Note-Taking Skills—The ability to take clear and complete notes is one of the most important aspects of academic listening. This part of the text guides students through the basics of effective note taking: writing down only key words, using abbreviations and symbols, and separating important ideas from inessential or irrelevant details.

Part 4: Listening For Pleasure—This part of the book is just for fun! Lessons are designed to build students' confidence in listening by presenting enjoyable, motivating topics and contexts, such as TV shows and stories. These lessons can be used at any time during the course to provide a change of pace and to show students that listening can be interesting and pleasurable.

Although the unit structure varies somewhat from part to part, most of the longer listenings follow this pattern:

Unit Warm Up: These activities activate students' prior knowledge of the topic.

Before You Listen: This section includes a **Vocabulary Preview** which targets high-frequency, useful words from the listening text. In addition, students have an opportunity to predict the listening content.

While You Listen: Students listen and complete one or more tasks which practice what they learned in the Skill Presentation.

After You Listen: These activities integrate speaking to reinforce the target listening skills. Tasks are designed to stimulate discussion and critical thinking about issues raised in the listening.

A wide variety of topics are discussed in *Listening Power*. All were chosen to be engaging and of high interest to as many learners as possible.

The authors of the *Listening Power* series hope that both you and your students find this series useful and enjoyable.

To the Student

Welcome to Listening Power!

Listening is a very important language skill. Most people spend more time listening than they do speaking, reading, or writing. Listening is important in the classroom, at work, and in social situations. However, learning to listen in another language is quite a challenge. When you listen to an English-language TV show, movie, lecture, or just hear a conversation, you may feel overwhelmed and just "tune out."

The *Listening Power* series is designed to guide you through the process of improving your listening skills. You'll hear a wide variety of listening materials: sentences, short conversations, longer dialogs, lectures, and parts of radio and TV shows. As you listen, you'll complete a wide variety of practice activities:

- Completing comprehension exercises about the information you hear

- Learning to listen for main ideas and details and drawing inferences

- Building your vocabulary

- Understanding idiomatic English

- Understanding the organization of lectures

- Analyzing and discussing the ideas in lectures

- Taking notes while you listen to a lecture

- Evaluating and improving your notes

You will have opportunities to work individually, in pairs or small groups, and as a whole class. To get the most out of this course, when you listen, you need to relax and focus on just listening; try not to think of other things. It's also important that you fully participate in group activities and discussions.

Listening Power 3 is divided into four parts. Each part focuses on one important element of listening, so it is like four books in one. However, you do not have to complete the parts in order. You and your teacher are encouraged to move from part to part and from unit to unit and work on the skills that you and your classmates need the most.

Part 1: Language Focus—The units in this section focus on language skill areas that are often challenging for learners at the high-intermediate level: understanding reduced forms (such as "couldja" and "didja"), intonation patterns, and idioms. After each Skill Presentation, you will complete several practice activities. The Put It Together section at the end of the unit provides more practice with longer, more challenging listening.

Part 2: Comprehension Focus—This part has two sections. In **Building Skills,** you will listen to longer conversations and talks, and practice comprehension skills such as understanding main ideas, supporting ideas, and details; drawing inferences; distinguishing facts and opinions; and recognizing patterns of organization. The **Applying Skills** units offer interesting listening texts and additional practice activities to put your new listening skills into practice.

Part 3: Note-Taking Skills—This part of the text will help you learn the basics of effective note taking: writing down key words, using abbreviations and symbols, and separating important ideas from unimportant details. You will also take notes on a long lecture and evaluate and improve your note-taking skills.

Part 4: Listening For Pleasure—This part of the book is just for fun! These lessons present enjoyable topics such as listening to an old-time radio show and to stand-up comedy so that you can practice your listening skills while having fun at the same time.

To increase your skills, the authors recommend that you practice listening as much as possible and use your English whenever you can. Listen to radio shows and watch TV shows in English. Go to English-language movies. Take part in conversations in English. Visit websites that provide practice listening, such as those provided by the BBC© World Service, Voice of America: Learning English, radio shows on NPR®, and TED Talks.

We hope that you find this series useful and enjoyable.

Tammy LeRoi Gilbert
Bruce Rogers

PART 1

Language Focus

Understanding Reduced Forms

Unit Warm Up

🎧 *Read along as you listen to the advertisement. Notice how the underlined words and phrases are pronounced.*

Genki Cha Green Tea Diet Drink

Do you <u>want to</u> lose <u>a lot of</u> weight fast? Check out our new green tea diet drink, Genki Cha. It's not just another boring diet drink. Not only is Genki Cha delicious, but it really works. So, don't say you "<u>should have</u>" when you "<u>could have</u>." <u>Come on</u>, it's easy. Just email us with <u>your</u> mailing address and we'll send <u>you</u> some free samples. Start <u>drinking</u> up and <u>slimming</u> down the healthy way.

AN ANCIENT WAY TO BETTER HEALTH

SKILL PRESENTATION

When English speakers are talking naturally and quickly, they often use the reduced (shortened) forms of words. This means they don't pronounce every word clearly, and sometimes two or more words are connected to sound like a single word. We use reduced forms when we speak, but we don't usually use them when we write. This is especially true for academic or business communication, in which the reduced form is considered incorrect.

Because reduced forms are so common, it's important to learn them so you can recognize and understand them when you are listening. This section will give you practice listening to and understanding some of the most common reduced forms.

Greetings

We often use reduced forms when we greet people or meet friends in casual situations. We use these forms to ask people about what they have been doing or how they are feeling.

> **Note**
> The *g* is frequently dropped on words ending in *-ing* and is pronounced as "in."

🎧 *Listen and repeat the full forms and their reduced forms.*

Saying hello		Saying good-bye	
Good morning	→ *G'mornin*	See you.	→ *Seeya.*
How is it going?	→ *Howzitgoin'?*	Good-bye.	→ *G'bye.*
What's up?	→ *Wassup?*	Good night.	→ *G'night.*

☑ **Check Yourself**

A. Practice the conversation with a partner. Try to use the reduced forms of the underlined phrases.

> **A:** Hey, John, <u>what's up</u>?
>
> **B:** Well, I've been looking for a job. <u>How is it going</u> with you?
>
> **A:** Everything's OK. I just got a new roommate.
>
> **B:** Well, I better get <u>going</u>. (See note on page 2.)
>
> **A:** OK, <u>see you</u> later.
>
> **B:** <u>Good-bye</u>.

B. Now say hello to the people around you. Use reduced forms for the greetings. Have a short conversation. Then say good-bye.

Phrases with *a, of,* and *to*

Some of the most common reduced forms include short words like *a* and *of.* In these reduced forms, both *a* and *of* are generally pronounced "uh" (/ə/).

🎧 *Listen and repeat the full forms and their reduced forms.*

Phrases with *a*		Phrases with *of*		Phrases with *to*	
get a	→ *gedda*	a lot of	→ *alodda*	going to	→ *gonna*
such a	→ *sucha*	kind of	→ *kinda*	has to	→ *hasta*
what a	→ *whadda*	out of	→ *oudda*	have to	→ *hafta*
		some of	→ *somma*	want to	→ *wanna*
		sort of	→ *sorda*	used to	→ *useta*

🎧 *Listen. Do you hear the reduced form or the full form of the words in bold? Check (✓) your answers.*

	Reduced	Full
1. **What a** great movie!	☐	☐
2. I **want to** learn how to speak Italian.	☐	☐
3. There are **a lot of** people on the beach today.	☐	☐
4. What **kind of** classes are you taking this term?	☐	☐
5. When do you **have to** start your new job?	☐	☐
6. We need to go shopping because we're **out of** milk.	☐	☐

Questions

We frequently reduce words and combinations of sounds when we ask questions.

> **Note**
> When you ask questions that begin with an auxiliary verb + a pronoun (*did you, do you,* etc.) or when you ask *wh-*questions with auxiliary verbs (*what/when/where did you,* etc.), *you* is generally pronounced as *ja* or *ya*.

🎧 *Listen and repeat the full forms and their reduced forms.*

Did/Do + *you*	Wh- words + *you*	Could/Would + *you*
Do you want to …? → *yawanna/ jawanna*	What do you …? → *whaddaya*	Could you …? → *couldja*
Did you eat …? → *j'eat*	Where did you …? → *wheredja*	Would you …? → *wouldja*
Did you ever …? → *j'ever*	When did you …? → *whendja*	

☑ **Check Yourself**

🎧 *Listen. Complete the questions with the full forms from the list above.*

1. A: _____ think we should do today?

   B: Well, I think it would be fun to take a long hike.

2. A: _____ water the plants tomorrow?

   B: Sure, no problem.

3. A: _____ find your glasses?

   B: Yeah, I left them in the car.

4. **A:** _____ buy that beautiful coat?

   B: I got it at a small shop downtown.

5. **A:** _____ travel in South America?

   B: I was there last year.

6. **A:** _____ have chicken or fish for dinner?

   B: Actually, I'd like to call and have a pizza delivered.

Other Common Reductions

Some other types of reductions include words that are shortened by leaving out sounds and words that are combined to sound like one word.

🎧 *Listen and repeat the full forms and their reduced forms.*

Shortened Words				Combined Words		
about	→	*'bout*	him	→	*'im*	bet you	→	*becha*
around	→	*'round*	suppose	→	*s'pose*	come on	→	*c'mon*
because	→	*cuz*	your	→	*yer*	don't know	→	*dunno*
her	→	*'er*				used to	→	*usta*

☑ **Check Yourself**

🎧 *Listen. Does the speaker use the reduced form of the words in bold? Check (✓) Yes or No.*

	Yes	No
1. I asked **her** to join us for dinner tonight.	☐	☐
2. I **don't know** where we're meeting today.	☐	☐
3. I **suppose** we could take a different road if Highway 1 is closed.	☐	☐
4. Where did you leave **your** coat?	☐	☐
5. The flight will be delayed **because** of bad weather.	☐	☐
6. Oh, **come on!** That can't be true.	☐	☐
7. I'm not sure, but I think his house is **around** here somewhere.	☐	☐
8. Please tell **him** that the prices have increased by 10 percent.	☐	☐

Modal + *have*

The word *have* is often reduced when it follows modals, such as *should*, *could*, or *might*.

🎧 *Listen and repeat the full forms and their reduced forms.*

Modal + *have*			
must have	→ *musta*	could have	→ *coulda*
might have	→ *mighta*	should have	→ *shoulda*
		would have	→ *woulda*

☑ Check Yourself

🎧 *Listen. Complete the sentences with the full forms of the modal + have.*

1. I _____would have_____ called you, but my cell phone wasn't working.

2. Traffic is stopped, so there _____ been a car accident.

3. I _____ taken the bus instead of driving in this rainstorm.

4. Sam _____ left his coat in the restaurant.

5. You _____ borrowed the book from me.

6. It _____ been better to talk to your boss before you left.

PRACTICE

■ EXERCISE 1

🎧 *Listen. Underline all of the reduced forms you hear.*

1. Well, good night. I'll see you at work tomorrow.

2. I bet you that John will win the race.

3. She might have gotten on the wrong bus.

4. I need to get a new cell phone because I lost mine.

5. Do you want to have soup or salad with dinner?

6. I suppose I could have cleaned the house, but I was feeling sort of lazy yesterday.

7. Where did you find such a nice hat?

8. Come on! Would you just ask her to come to the party?

9. Did you ever talk to Mary? She knows a lot of people who could help you.

10. You should have told me you were going to pick me up at the airport.

11. What are you going to do about that hole in your floor?

12. I don't know where James used to live. Could you ask him?

■ EXERCISE 2

🎧 *Listen to each question. Check (✓) the best response.*

1. a. ☐ Sounds good to me.   b. ☐ It's tomorrow.

2. a. ☐ I'm doing OK.   b. ☐ I'm taking the bus.

3. a. ☐ No, I haven't heard anything.   b. ☐ No, I didn't have time.

4. a. ☐ I went to Italy.   b. ☐ About a week ago.

5. a. ☐ Yes, it was on sale.   b. ☐ Sure, I'll pick some up.

6. a. ☐ No, I didn't arrive too early.   b. ☐ Of course, I was really late.

7. a. ☐ I said I'd open it in a minute.   b. ☐ On the living room table.

8. a. ☐ No, I'm going home.   b. ☐ No, I didn't.

9. a. ☐ No, but I'd like to.   b. ☐ Yes, it looks like so much fun.

10. a. ☐ He always forgets to call.   b. ☐ He should be here soon.

■ EXERCISE 3

A. 🎧 *Listen. Complete the conversations with the full forms of the missing words or phrases.*

Conversation 1

A: Hello?

B: Hi, Nina, this is Brian. I'm so sorry to be calling you so late. Sounds like I must have woken you up.

A: Yes, you did. It's midnight here in New York City.
   You _____ called a little earlier. So, what's up?
        (1)

B: I'm so sorry. I _____ called earlier, but my flight from San
        (2)
   Francisco has been delayed.

A: With all the thunderstorms, I _____ known you'd have trouble
        (3)
   getting here. Do you know how much longer you'll be delayed?

B: I don't know for sure, but _____ the airline agents are saying
        (4)
   we might not be able to fly out until tomorrow morning.

A: Well, _____ want to do if that happens?
        (5)

B: I guess I'll _____ check into a hotel for the night.   *(continued)*
        (6)

A: OK, _____ call me in the morning to let me know when you'll
(7)

   arrive?

B: I'll do that. Get some sleep.

A. You too. _____ .
(8)

Conversation 2

A: _____ . I didn't see you around the office yesterday.
(1)

B: Yeah, I should have told you I'd be _____ the office.
(2)

A: So, come on, tell me. _____ go?
(3)

B: Well, I _____ already know.
(4)

A: Hmm, I can't guess. _____ just tell me already?
(5)

B: OK, I went to a job interview. Don't say anything to our supervisor because I

   don't want _____ to know.
(6)

A: Don't worry; I'm _____ keeping a secret.
(7)

B: You're such a good friend. _____ go to lunch today so I can tell
(8)

   you all about it?

A: Absolutely! _____ think we should leave?
(9)

B: Um, how_____ 1:00?
(10)

A: OK, _____ then.
(11)

B. **Work with a partner. Practice the conversations in Exercise A. Try to use the reduced forms.**

■ **EXERCISE 4**

A. *Complete these questions with your own ideas. Try to use reduced forms.*

1. Where did you _____?

2. What do you want to _____?

3. What would you have _____?

4. Should you have _____?

5. Are you going to _____?

6. Could you _____?

B. Work with a partner. Ask and answer the questions you wrote in Exercise A. Use reduced forms.

Example
....

> *A:* **Whaddya wanna** *study in college?*
>
> *B:* **I wanna** *study history.*

PUT IT TOGETHER

■ EXERCISE 1

Roommates: Establishing "House Rules"

It's not unusual for a group of people living together to establish "house rules." House rules are generally a list of things that roommates agree to do or not to do while living in a house or sharing an apartment. Having these rules can make living together easier for everyone. However, there can be problems if not everyone follows the rules. When this happens, it is important for the roommates to get together and discuss solutions.

A. Vocabulary Preview *Match the words to their definitions. Use a dictionary if necessary. Then use the words to complete the sentences below.*

_e_ 1. Whoops!	a. expression used to tell someone that something you said was not important
_____ 2. chore	b. put on top of one another in a messy way
_____ 3. react	c. find a solution to a problem
_____ 4. never mind	d. make someone angry or annoyed
_____ 5. ignore	e. expression of surprise at making a mistake
_____ 6. piled up	f. a job that you have to do regularly
_____ 7. work [it] out	g. not pay attention to something on purpose
_____ 8. irritate	h. respond by showing how something makes you feel

9. _____, it doesn't matter what I think.

10. The neighbor's dogs _____ me when they bark all night long.

11. So many books were _____ on the desk that they fell on the floor.

12. Don't _____ the teacher. Please listen because she has something important to say.

13. John, the only _____ you have to do is wash the dishes after dinner.

14. _____ I forgot to pick up the milk you asked me to buy.

15. I know you're worried, but it will be OK. We'll find a way to _____.

16. How did Jody _____ when she found out she didn't get the job?

B. 🎧 *Listen. Three roommates are talking about house rules. Complete the conversation with the full forms of the missing words and phrases.*

> **Useful Terms**
> **fridge:** a common reduction for the word *refrigerator*
> **OJ:** a common abbreviation for *orange juice*

Ellen: Hi, everyone. _____(1)?

Susan: Yeah, I _____(2) you're wondering why I asked you to get together this evening, right? Well, I think it might be good if we had a talk about the house rules _____(3) I feel like we've started to ignore them. Please let me explain _____(4) the problems I've noticed recently. First, we all agreed that we have to wash our dishes when we're done eating, right? Unfortunately, I'm finding _____(5) dishes piled up in the kitchen sink. Sorry to be reacting this way, but I'm sort of irritated about that. And another thing …

Jenny: Excuse me, Susan, but I _____(6) ask you something. _____(7) find the dirty dishes?

Susan: Well, Jenny, let's see … it _____(8) been last week that I actually started noticing them.

Jenny: Sorry, Susan, I always _____(9) do my dishes right after I ate, but … um … lately, I've been really busy, so I might have left them in the sink for a while.

Susan: You _____(10) said something because I would have helped you out with your chores around the house. _____(11) try to talk to me about things like this next time?

Ellen: Uh, since we're talking _____(12) these kinds of things … oh, never mind …

Jenny: _____ say something, Ellen? _____; don't be
(13)   (14)

afraid to speak up. Everyone _____ have a chance to talk.
(15)

Ellen: Well, OK then. It's _____ been bothering me ... um, I
(16)

think somebody has been drinking my orange juice.

Susan: Whoops! It _____ been me because I have some OJ in
(17)

the fridge, too. I think we drink the same kind, but I usually keep

mine on the top shelf. _____ put yours?
(18)

Ellen: I don't know for sure, but _____ think we should do to
(19)

keep our OJ separate?

Jenny: I have an idea. How about writing _____ names on the
(20)

OJ cartons? I bet you that will solve the problem. _____
(21)

that might work?

Susan: What a great idea! I'm going to go and _____ red marker
(22)

right now. I'm so glad we could work this out!

C. 🎧 *Listen to parts of the conversation. Circle the correct answers to the questions.*

1. What does Susan say they all agreed to do according to the house rules?

   a. not worry about using a lot of dishes

   b. wash their dishes after they eat

   c. pile their dishes in the sink

2. How is Susan feeling about the situation?

   a. irritated

   b. sorry

   c. surprised

3. Why does Jenny say that she might have left her dishes in the sink lately?

   a. She was ignoring her house chores.

   b. She was gone for a while last week.

   c. She has been busy recently.

4. What does Susan ask Jenny to do the next time?

   a. talk to her if Jenny needs help

   b. do her house chores in the future

   (continued)

   c. let Susan find someone to help

5. Why do you think Jenny says to Ellen, "Do you want to say something, Ellen?"

   a. because Ellen isn't paying attention

   b. because Ellen hasn't spoken yet

   c. because Ellen seems to be afraid to express her feelings

6. Why does Susan say she might have drunk Ellen's OJ?

   a. because she drank the OJ on the top shelf

   b. because they both drink the same kind of OJ

   c. because she didn't know where her OJ was

7. What does Jenny think they should do about the problem?

   a. put their OJ in different places

   b. buy more OJ for each other

   c. write their names on the OJ cartons

8. What does Susan say she is going do at the end of the conversation?

   a. get a marking pen

   b. buy some OJ

   c. wait for Ellen to get back

D. *Compare your answers with a partner. Then check them with your teacher.*

■ EXERCISE 2

A. *Work in a group. Ask and answer the questions. Use the reduced forms of the underlined words.*

1. Do you have to do a lot of chores around your house? Could you give me some examples of things you have to do?

2. What do you think roommates have to do to make sure everyone gets along well?

3. Do you think it's a good idea to make house rules? Why or why not?

4. Did you ever have a problem with a roommate or a family member you lived with? When did you have this problem? Why did you have this problem? (Answers should include because.)

5. What are some of the things you could have done to avoid the problem? (Answers should include might have, could have, or should have.)

6. What do you suppose is the most common problem roommates have with each other?

B. *Work with your group. Imagine that you are roommates. Come up with a list of house rules. Then share your ideas with the class.*

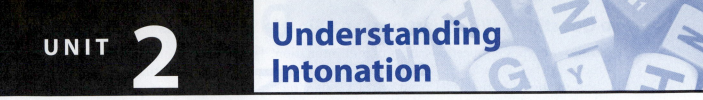

Understanding Intonation

Unit Warm Up

🎧 *Listen to the conversations. Pay attention to the second speaker's response. How is that speaker feeling? Number the pictures from 1 to 4 to match each speaker to a picture.*

a _____

b _____

c _____

d _____

SKILL PRESENTATION

When you heard the responses in the Unit Warm Up, how did you know what the speakers were feeling? The rising or falling intonation in their voices was most likely your clue. Intonation helps to create the "music" of language. It refers to the way that the level or pitch of your voice falls or rises when you speak. We use intonation every time we speak to provide and ask for specific information or to express our feelings. Understanding intonation is essential for interpreting the meaning of what people are really saying to you.

In this unit you will learn what each kind of intonation means, and you will have a chance to practice listening to intonation patterns in different structures and expressions.

Yes/No Questions, Wh- Questions, and Simple Statements

Different types of questions use different intonation. Typically, our voice rises a little at the end when we ask a *yes/no* question. The speaker expects an answer that begins with "yes" or "no." On the other hand, when asking a *wh-* question, our voice goes down at the end. In this case, the speaker is expecting a longer, more detailed answer.

A. 🎧 *Listen and repeat the questions.*

Yes/No Questions	Wh- Questions
1. Do you have time for a cup of coffee?	1. How do I turn this machine off?
2. Could we meet you at the restaurant?	2. What's going to happen to him?
3. Would you mind if I left early?	3. When will her flight be arriving?

Like *wh-* questions, simple statements fall at the end. However, it is common to turn a statement into a *yes/no* question just by making your voice go up at the end.

B. 🎧 *Listen and repeat the statements and questions.*

Statement	Question
1. We don't have any milk left.	We don't have any milk left?
2. They can't schedule a meeting this week.	They can't schedule a meeting this week?

> **Note**
> It is common to use a simple statement with rising intonation when we are asking for confirmation of something we already think is true.
>
> **Example**
> ....
>
> Q: You visited your family this weekend?　　A: Yes, that's right.

☑ **Check Yourself**

🎧 *Listen. Do you hear a statement or a question? Check (✓) your answer.*

	Statement	Question			Statement	Question
1.	☐	☐		5.	☐	☐
2.	☐	☐		6.	☐	☐
3.	☐	☐		7.	☐	☐
4.	☐	☐		8.	☐	☐

Tag Questions

The intonation in tag questions depends on whether the speaker is sure (or unsure) about what he or she is asking. We use tag questions in the following ways.

Falling Intonation

- To make sure that something is **correct**:

Example

You finished your homework, didn't you?

Rising Intonation

- To **ask for information** from the listener when we are unsure about something:

Example

You're Greg's sister, aren't you?

🎧 *Listen and repeat the questions.*

Tag Questions: Sure

1. You always know the shortest way to get home, don't you?

2. Exercising early is the best way to start the day, isn't it?

3. You're not feeling too well, are you?

Tag Questions: Unsure

1. You know the way to get home, don't you?

2. That's your boss sitting over there, isn't it?

3. You're not going to Dan's party, are you?

☑ Check Yourself

A. 🎧 **Listen. Mark the end of the sentence with falling intonation (⌢↘) or rising intonation (⌣↗).**

1. That was a great movie, wasn't it?

2. Lena is studying Spanish, isn't she?

3. New York City can be unbelievably cold in the winter, can't it?

4. They eat dinner in restaurants a lot, don't they?

5. You're going to travel to Italy when you're in Europe, aren't you?

B. 🎧 *Listen. Is the speaker sure or unsure? Circle the correct answers.*

1. sure   not sure   4. sure   not sure

2. sure   not sure   5. sure   not sure

3. sure   not sure   6. sure   not sure

Alternative Questions

An alternative question includes two or more answer choices (alternatives) within the question itself. When choices are being offered, the intonation rises on the first choice(s) and then falls on the second or last choice.

A. 🎧 *Listen and repeat the questions.*

Alternative Questions: Choice

Should I call Jim on the phone or should I talk to him in person? (You should talk to him in person.)

Are you leaving because it's too noisy or because you're tired? (Because I'm really tired.)

Do you want to spend the afternoon shopping, visiting museums, or walking in the park? (I'd like to go for a walk in the park.)

Some questions may look like alternative questions which ask for a choice but the expected answer is *yes* or *no*. The intonation in these questions rises at the end of the question.

B. 🎧 *Listen and repeat the questions.*

Alternative Questions: Yes/No

Could you make the reservations for 7:00 or 7:30 at the latest? (Yes, I think we can all make it around that time.)

Do you have any brothers or sisters living in the area? (No, my brother and my sisters live in different parts of the country.)

Did you get any phone messages or emails from the company? (Yes, they called and they emailed too.)

🎧 *Listen. Which type of alternative question do you hear—choice or yes/no? Check (✓) Choice or Yes/No.*

	Choice	Yes/No			Choice	Yes/No
1.	☐	☐		4.	☐	☐
2.	☐	☐		5.	☐	☐
3.	☐	☐		6.	☐	☐

Changing Meaning: Modals and Linking Verbs

The meaning of statements can be changed if the speaker uses rising intonation for specific words that don't normally rise. This is especially true when the intonation rises on modals (*could, might, should, would*, etc.) or the *be* verb and verbs of perception (*be, seem, feel, look, sound*, etc.): It creates the opposite meaning.

Example

He appears to be sleeping. (*He is probably sleeping.*)

He appears to be sleeping. (*He is not really sleeping.*)

🎧 **Listen and repeat the statements.**

Rising intonation with modals and linking verbs

We should eat more vegetables and fruit (*but we don't*).

It looks like a real diamond (*but it isn't*).

She seems to be happy (*but she isn't*).

He was a good student (*but he isn't now*).

✓ **Check Yourself**

🎧 *Listen to the conversations. Check (✓) True or False for each statement.*

		True	False
1.	They turned the heat off in the building.	☐	☐
2.	Susan will get help with her homework today.	☐	☐
3.	Jim's parents are going to London next week.	☐	☐
4.	Meg gets enough sleep at night.	☐	☐
5.	Kathy likes her new job a lot.	☐	☐
6.	It is possible that Steve will get an invitation to the party.	☐	☐

Understanding Emotions

Words and Short Phrases

We can change the function or emotional meaning of a word or phrase simply by changing our intonation. In fact, a speaker can change the meaning of almost any word or phrase by changing the intonation. You've already learned about two types of intonation—rising and falling—but there are a few others that help us to express our emotions: high-rising ↑ and flat ⟶ (no rising, no falling).

> **Note**
> For *yes/no* questions, we use rising intonation. However, to express certain feelings, we make our voice rise even higher. We use this "high rise" intonation to express strong feelings, such as complete disbelief or surprise. We also use high rise intonation to contradict or to request clarification.

A. 🎧 **Listen. Notice the different intonation patterns.**

High-rising intonation

↑

Really? You ran six miles? (meaning: "I'm surprised you ran so far!")

↑

Great! We get an extra day of paid vacation this year. (meaning: "I'm so happy we get more paid vacation this year!")

Flat intonation (no rising, no falling)

⟶

Really. How surprising that the prices for airline tickets went up again. (meaning: "I'm not surprised at all that prices for airline tickets increased; I expected it.")

⟶

Great. Since our car isn't working, we'll get some exercise bicycling to work. (meaning: "I'm not really happy about bicycling to work; I'd rather drive.")

> **Useful Term**
> **sarcasm:** using your voice to show that what you say is the opposite of what you really mean in order to make an unkind joke or to show that you are annoyed

B. 🎧 **Listen and practice.**

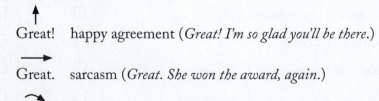

↑

Great!   happy agreement (*Great! I'm so glad you'll be there.*)

⟶

Great.   sarcasm (*Great. She won the award, again.*)

⤴

Great.   disappointment (*Great. Another rainy day.*)

↑
Really?   surprise (*Really? You're getting married?*)

⌒⌒
Really?   disagreement; disbelief (*Really? That's not what I heard.*)

↑
Come on!   asking please; pleading (*Come on! Please let me borrow your car.*)

⌒⌒
Come on.   disbelief (*Oh, come on. That didn't really happen.*)

⌒
Come on.   worried or nervous (*Come on. We're going to be late.*)

↑
Yeah!   strongly agree (*Yeah! I'd love to win a free vacation.*)

⌒⌒
Yeah, right.   agreement/realization (*Yeah, right. It's a perfect solution.*)

⌒⌒
Yeah, right.   disagree; sarcasm (*Yeah, right. Losing your job is a good thing.*)

☑ Check Yourself

A. 🎧 **Listen. You will hear a word or a short phrase followed by a sentence. Circle the intonation you hear for the words in bold.**

1. **Yeah, right**   ⌒⌒   ⌒⌒

2. **Come on**   ⌒⌒   ⌒⌒

3. **Really**   ↑   ⌒

4. **Great**   →   ⌒

5. **Come on**   ⌒⌒   ⌒   ↑

6. **Really**   ↑   ⌒⌒   ⌒⌒

B. 🎧 **Listen again. Circle the word that describes the feeling that each speaker expresses.**

1. disbelief   agreement   surprise
2. disbelief   agreement   worried
3. agreement   surprise   sarcasm
4. worried   agreement   sarcasm
5. disbelief   agreement   worried
6. disbelief   surprise   agreement

Short Phrases and Sentences

As you have seen, we use different levels or patterns of pitch to express specific emotions. This is a good starting point for understanding how other people feel. However, emotional expression also depends on other factors of speech, such as volume, speed, length of response, and quality of voice (warm or cold tone). The meaning of what we say also depends on context or the situation at the moment.

A. 🎧 *Listen to the intonation patterns in these sentences. Read the explanations of the contexts.*

Good luck! (context: speaker is hopeful = wishing someone luck)

Good luck. (context: speaker is not hopeful; doubtful = results might not be lucky)

How are you? (context: talking to someone you see often = neutral/unemotional)

How are you? (context: talking to someone who is sick or upset = concerned)

What are you doing? (context: asking a question = neutral/unemotional)

What are you doing? (context: speaker knows what you are doing = anger, disapproval, or surprise)

What are you doing? (context: speaker doesn't know what you are doing = anger, disapproval, or surprise)

B. 🎧 *Listen again and repeat the sentences.*

☑ Check Yourself

🎧 *Listen. Pay attention to the context and the speakers' intonation. Circle the feeling that each speaker expresses.*

1. anger   surprise   doubt

2. surprise   disbelief   concern

3. anger   surprise   disappointment

4. doubt   happiness   surprise

5. disappointment   surprise   concern

6. sarcasm   anger   no emotion

7. concern   surprise   happiness

8. sarcasm   surprise   disbelief

9. surprise   sarcasm   happiness

10. concern   anger   no emotion

PRACTICE

■ **EXERCISE 1**

> **Note**
> Sometimes, even with very little information, you can understand a lot by listening to a speaker's intonation patterns. You will practice this in Exercises 1 and 2.

A. 🎧 *Listen to the conversation. Use the intonation to help you understand what the speakers mean. Mark the intonation of each line of the conversation with arrows:*

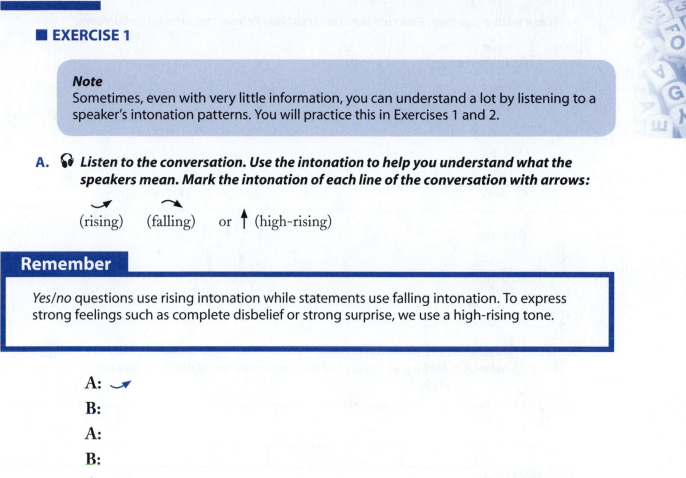

(rising)   (falling)   or ↑ (high-rising)

Remember

Yes/no questions use rising intonation while statements use falling intonation. To express strong feelings such as complete disbelief or strong surprise, we use a high-rising tone.

A: ↗

B:

A:

B:

A:

B:

B. 🎧 *Listen again. Try to guess what the situation is (where the speakers are and what they are doing) and how Speaker B is feeling at the end of the conversation. Write your guesses.*

Situation: _____

Speaker B (feeling): _____

■ EXERCISE 2

A. *Work with a partner. Practice the conversation. Follow the intonation arrows.*

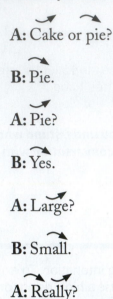

A: Cake or pie?

B: Pie.

A: Pie?

B: Yes.

A: Large?

B: Small.

A: Really?

B. *Try to guess what the situation is (where the speakers are and what they are doing) and how Speaker A is feeling at the end of the conversation. Write your guesses.*

Situation: _____

Speaker A (feeling): _____

■ EXERCISE 3

A. 🎧 *Listen to the conversation. Mark the intonation of each of the underlined words and phrases with arrows:*

(rising)   (falling)   or ↑ (high-rising)

Man:	Aren't you <u>thirsty</u>?
Woman:	<u>Yeah</u>. Should we get something to <u>drink</u>?
Man:	<u>Sure</u>. Do you want to <u>go to a café</u>, or should we just <u>get a bottle of water</u>?
Woman:	Let's go to a <u>café</u>. <u>The place that has coffee</u> or <u>the juice bar</u>?
Man:	Well, I guess we <u>should</u> go to the juice bar, but I want some coffee, <u>don't you</u>?
Woman:	Oh, <u>come on</u>. I love the juice bar. Can we go <u>there</u>? <u>Please</u>?
Man:	<u>OK</u> ... if you really want to...

B. Check your answers to Exercise A with your teacher. Then answer these questions. Write Y for Yes or N for No.

1. _____ Does the man give a choice between going to a café and buying water?

2. _____ Does the woman agree to go to a café?

3. _____ Does the man want to go to the place that has coffee?

4. _____ Does the man give a choice between coffee or tea?

5. _____ Does the man want to go to the juice bar?

C. Work with a partner. Practice the conversation in Exercise A. Use the correct intonation patterns.

◼ EXERCISE 4

🎧 *Listen. Check (✓) the best response.*

1. a. ☐ Thank you!   b. ☐ Well, at least I can try.

2. a. ☐ The train. It will be faster. b. ☐ Yes, the train is faster.

3. a. ☐ Do you really think so?   b. ☐ No, the kind I like is smaller.

4. a. ☐ I'm on my way to the library. b. ☐ Sorry, is there a problem?

5. a. ☐ Yes, I think he is.   b. ☐ What do you think is wrong?

6. a. ☐ OK, I'll try to run.   b. ☐ No, my feet are hurting.

7. a. ☐ I don't really know.   b. ☐ Yeah, he has won lots of awards.

8. a. ☐ I'm fine. How are you?   b. ☐ I'm getting better every day.

9. a. ☐ What's the matter with that?   b. ☐ OK, I will if you like them so much.

10. a. ☐ You're right. Do you want to read it?   b. ☐ No, I still have a few pages to read.

Work with a partner. Create your own conversation using the intonation patterns you've just learned. Include different types of questions and use expressions, such as really, good luck, yeah, right, or how are you?

Example

Karen: How are you, Bill?

Bill: Oh, hello, Karen. I'm doing well, thanks. I just started my new job.

Karen: Really? I guess you weren't too happy with your old job, were you?

Bill: I liked the work, but the pay wasn't great.

Karen: Well, good luck with your new job!

PUT IT TOGETHER

■ EXERCISE 1

Radio "Call-In" Show

A "call-in show" is a radio program during which listeners call the radio station to discuss issues or ask questions during the show. Sometimes the host of the show interviews a guest, and callers phone in to ask the guest questions.

In this exercise, you are going to listen to a radio call-in show called "Ask a Scientist." Callers ask the show's guest, Dr. Patrick Lane, questions about recent discoveries on the planet Mars.

A. Vocabulary Preview *Read each sentence. Then circle the best definition for the underlined word(s).*

1. The water in the pond was so <u>shallow</u> that it came only up to our knees.

   a. a short distance from the top to the bottom

   b. a short distance from side to side

2. After the professor explained his theory in detail, it sounded more realistic and seemed more <u>plausible</u>.

   a. unlikely

   b. believable

3. The Internet is one of the most <u>significant</u> technologies of the 20th century.

   a. unusual

   b. very important

4. Their mother promised the children ice cream after dinner to <u>motivate</u> them to eat their vegetables.

   a. encourage

   b. force

5. Martha is <u>skeptical</u> that Stuart will be on time because he is always late.

    a. unclear   **b.** doubtful

6. Did the company <u>promote</u> the product on television or in the newspaper?

    a. make known to the public   **b.** offer at a cheap price

7. Jeff stepped on a sharp rock in the river because it was <u>submerged</u> and he didn't see it.

    a. under the water   **b.** broken into pieces

8. Eating too many fatty foods can have negative <u>implications</u>, such as weight gain and poor overall health.

    a. reason   **b.** possible result

B. 🎧 *Listen to the first part of a radio call-in show. Pay attention to the speakers' intonation and take notes on a separate piece of paper. Write any words or phrases in which the speakers use intonation to express emotion.*

> **Useful Terms**
> **microbe:** an extremely small living creature, such as a virus that cannot be seen without a microscope
> **ripples:** small, low waves or series of gentle waves across a liquid surface

C. *Compare your notes with a partner.*

D. 🎧 *Listen again to parts of the radio show. Circle (a) or (b) based on the speakers' intonation.*

1. a. no emotion   b. concerned
2. a. sure   b. unsure
3. a. sarcasm   b. strong agreement
4. a. surprise   b. disbelief
5. a. strong agreement   b. sarcasm
6. a. said   b. did not say
7. a. agreement/realization   b. disagreement
8. a. sure   b. unsure
9. a. question   b. statement
10. a. yes/no   b. choice
11. a. agreement   b. disappointment

■ EXERCISE 2

A. 🎧 *Listen to the final part of the radio call-in show. Notice the caller's questions and intonation. Listen for Dr. Lane's answers. Take notes if necessary.*

B. *Read the questions. Circle the correct answers.*

1. Why is the discovery of water so significant according to Dr. Lane?

   a. because it's important for life on Earth

   b. because it means life could have existed on Mars

   c. because it's essential for planets to exist

2. What does the caller, Jean, think about what Dr. Lane is saying?

   a. She's excited about what he is saying and wants to hear more.

   b. She's in a hurry to get off the phone and doesn't care about what he is saying.

   c. She's doubtful and doesn't believe what he is saying is true.

3. What does Dr. Lane say is probably true if any signs of microbes are found on Mars?

   a. There may be life on many other planets.

   b. It proves water exists on the planet surface.

   c. It will motivate us to find other living creatures.

4. How does Dr. Lane answer Sylvia's question, "During your lectures, are people usually excited about the possibility of life on other planets, or are they skeptical?"

   a. He says some people are excited but others are skeptical.

   b. He says people are usually excited about the Mars discovery.

   c. He says most people are not hopeful about finding life on other planets.

C. *Work in a group. Discuss these questions. Use intonation to express different emotions, such as surprise, disagreement, sarcasm, and doubt or disbelief. Try to use responses such as* **come on, really, yeah, yeah right,** *and* **great.**

Example

····· ·····

> *A: Do you think there is life on other planets?*
>
> *B: Yeah, I really do think there is life on other planets.*
>
> *C: Yeah, right. I suppose you think aliens will visit Earth someday.*

1. What do you think about the discovery of water on Mars?

2. Do you believe that there could have been life on Mars in the past? Why or why not?

3. Do you think they will find living creatures on Mars in the future? Why or why not?

4. Do you think there is life on other planets? Why or why not?

Unit Warm Up

A. Look at the pictures and try to guess the meanings of the expressions (idioms). Write your guesses under the pictures. Then compare your answers with a partner.

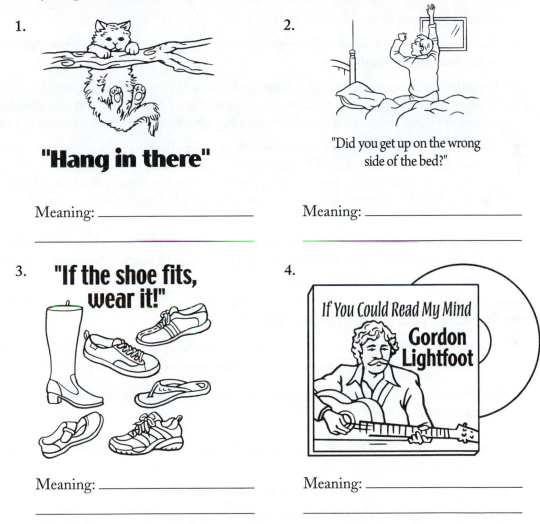

1.

"Hang in there"

Meaning: _____

_____

2.

"Did you get up on the wrong side of the bed?"

Meaning: _____

_____

3.

"If the shoe fits, wear it!"

Meaning: _____

_____

4.

If You Could Read My Mind
Gordon Lightfoot

Meaning: _____

_____

B. 🎧 Listen to people using the idioms from Exercise A. Match each idiom to its meaning.

_____ Speaker 1   a. accept something if it applies to you

_____ Speaker 2   b. guess what someone else is thinking

_____ Speaker 3   c. keep trying and don't give up when something is difficult or stressful

_____ Speaker 4   d. wake up and start the day in a bad mood and continue to be easily irritated

SKILL PRESENTATION

Idioms are phrases and sentences that have a special meaning. Every language has idioms, and idioms can tell us a lot about a culture. It may be a challenge to learn them, but it is worth the effort. Learning and using idioms is a fun and colorful way to expand your English.

As you learned in the Unit Warm Up, the separate words in idioms, when combined, can have a very different meaning from their usual meaning. That means that even if you know every word you see or hear in an idiom, you still may not understand the meaning. However, knowing the context or the situation in which the idiom is used usually helps.

For example, look at the idiom in bold:

*I had to ask Katie the same question twice before she realized I was talking to her. She really **has her head in the clouds** today!*

Obviously, people cannot really have their heads in the clouds, but if you use the context ("I had to ask Katie the same question twice before she …"), you can guess that the idiom means something about not listening or about being unaware of what is happening around you.

The context can also help you determine whether an idiom has a positive (good) or negative (not good) meaning. The fact that the speaker had to ask Katie the same question twice suggests that "having your head in the clouds" is a negative idiom. In addition, it's helpful to listen to the speaker's tone of voice to get a feeling for whether an idiom is positive or negative.

Learning idioms that are commonly used in specific situations can help you avoid confusing or embarrassing moments. In this unit you will practice listening to and using idioms in different contexts or situations.

Idioms for Everyday Communication

Idioms related to communication are especially useful to learn. They provide us with expressions for describing how we communicate with each other in everyday conversation.

A. *Read the idioms and their definitions. Then talk with a partner. Are there any similar idioms in your culture?*

[can't] **get a word in edgewise** – not having a chance to say anything because someone else is talking too much

get in touch with [someone] – to communicate with someone by telephone or in writing

hit the nail (right) on the head – to be right or to say exactly the right thing

make a point – to say something important

make small talk – to talk about everyday things rather than something personal or important

be out of touch with [someone] – to no longer be communicating with someone, having no information about someone

put words in [someone's] mouth – to say something for someone else without asking if it's OK

a slip of the tongue (noun phrase) – make a mistake by mispronouncing a word or saying something you didn't really mean to say

speak your mind – to say honestly and directly what you think about something

stay [or keep] in touch with [someone] – to continue communicating with someone over time; to know what they are currently doing

take the words out of [someone's] mouth – to say the words someone else was going to say before they do

talk [someone] into doing [something] – to persuade someone to do something that they don't want to do

B. **Work with a partner. Which idioms from Exercise A use these words or phrases? Complete the chart.**

in touch with	*get in touch with someone*
speak/talk	
mouth/tongue	
other idioms	

C. 🎧 *Some idioms can have either a negative or a positive meaning. Understanding the "feeling" of the idioms will help you learn to use them appropriately. Listen, then check (✓) Positive or Negative to indicate the feeling of each idiom. Use the context to help you.*

	Positive	**Negative**
1. stay in touch with [someone]	☐	☐
2. make a point	☐	☐
3. be out of touch with [someone]	☐	☐
4. hit the nail on the head	☐	☐
5. put words in [someone's] mouth	☐	☐
6. a slip of the tongue	☐	☐
7. speak your mind	☐	☐
8. [can't] get a word in edgewise	☐	☐

☑ **Check Yourself**

🎧 *Listen. Circle the definition of the idiom(s) in each conversation.*

1. *Make small talk* means _____.

   a. talk about everyday topics

   b. give personal information

2. *Speak your mind* means _____.

   a. think about what you want to say

   b. say directly what you think

(continued)

3. *Put words in* [someone's] *mouth* means _____.

    a. help someone to introduce a new topic

    b. speak for someone else

4. *[Can't] get a word in edgewise* means _____.

    a. having no chance to speak

    b. not speaking because you disagree

5. *Get in touch with* [someone] means _____.

    a. contact by telephone or in writing

    b. continue communicating over time

6. *A slip of the tongue* means _____.

    a. saying something clever

    b. saying something you didn't really mean to say

7. *Stay in touch with* [someone] means _____.

    a. continue communicating over time

    b. start communicating with a new person

8. *Be out of touch with* [someone] means _____.

    a. not understanding what someone said

    b. no longer communicating with someone

9. *Talk* [someone] *into doing* means _____.

    a. discuss something in detail

    b. persuade someone to do something

10. *Hit the nail on the head* means _____.

    a. say exactly the right thing

    b. say directly what you think

11. *Make a point* means _____.

    a. say something important

    b. talk about everyday topics

12. *Take the words out of* [someone's] *mouth* means _____.

    a. wait for someone else to speak

    b. say the same words someone else was going to say

Idioms Commonly Used in the Workplace

People use idioms in all kinds of situations. In this section, you will learn idioms that are often used in the workplace.

A. 🎧 **Listen to the sentences. Check (✓) Positive or Negative to indicate the "feeling" of each idiom. Use the context to help you.**

	Positive	Negative
1. be in the red	☐	☐
2. throw cold water on [something]	☐	☐
3. be in the black	☐	☐
4. give [someone] the green light	☐	☐
5. cut corners	☐	☐
6. get off to a flying start	☐	☐
7. pass the buck	☐	☐
8. think outside the box	☐	☐

B. **Read the sentences. Match each underlined idiom with the correct definition below. Use the context to help you.**

_____ 1. I don't want to <u>throw cold water on</u> your idea, but I just don't think it will work.

_____ 2. <u>Give Jim the green light</u> to make the presentation. He is definitely ready to do it tomorrow.

_____ 3. Don't <u>cut corners</u>! Please try to work harder and do the best job you can.

_____ 4. The company is <u>in the red</u>. We might have to close soon if we don't start making more money.

_____ 5. Vivian invented, designed, and helped to market the new product. She always <u>has her fingers in every pie</u>.

_____ 6. All the employees in this department will be happy. They are going to get a pay raise <u>across the board</u>.

_____ 7. We have to invent new software that is completely different from anything else on the market. So we will need to <u>think outside the box</u>.

_____ 8. Our electronics store can <u>get off to a flying start</u> by offering the popular new computer game on opening day.

_____ 9. It looks like we will <u>break even</u> this month. We spent as much on advertising as we made in sales.

_____ 10. Airline tickets to Hawaii are cheap this month, so <u>strike while the iron is hot</u> and book your vacation flight now.

_____ 11. Our business made a lot of money last month and is finally <u>in the black</u>. Now we will be able to pay the office rent.

_____ 12. You should have fixed the problem yourself. Don't <u>pass the buck</u> to your coworkers when you make a mistake.

a. not take responsibility for a problem; let other people take care of it

b. have a very successful beginning to something

c. losing money; unprofitable

d. be successful; make money

e. find innovative or creative ideas or solutions

f. do things badly or incompletely to reduce effort or save money

g. have expenses equal to profits; have money lost equal to money earned

h. discourage or not allow

i. be involved in many different things

j. give permission to go ahead with something

k. including everyone or everything

l. take advantage of an opportunity and do something at the best possible time

C. **Compare your answers with a partner. Then check your answers with your teacher.**

> **Note**
> *Across the board* is used in sentence 6 on page 31 as an adverb. However, it can also be used as an adjective, in which case it is hyphenated: *There was an **across-the-board** increase in the price of gasoline worldwide.*

☑ Check Yourself

Complete the sentences with these idioms. (You may need to change the verb tense or the pronoun.)

across the board	cut corners	pass the buck
be in the black	get off to a flying start	strike while the iron is hot
be in the red	give [someone] the green light	think outside the box
break even	have [someone's] fingers in every pie	throw cold water on

1. Nancy wants to <u>_have her fingers in every pie_</u>. She insisted on not only choosing the guest speakers and contacting them but also creating a list of questions to ask them.

2. Usually the boss is busy, but right now he seems to be relaxed and happy. You should _____ and ask him if you can have the day off from work tomorrow.

3. Why don't you want me to start my own business? As usual, you always _____ all my dreams for success.

4. Unfortunately, our organization _____. We have been losing money for the past six months.

5. The company's website just went up an hour ago and, so far, it's had 4,000 visitors. I'd say that they _____.

6. None of the solutions you offered were very creative. Please _____ and present me with some more original ideas tomorrow.

7. After years of cutting costs, we can now start expanding because our business _____.

8. Did you hear that this airline is going to charge money for water _____? This new fee includes all its flights everywhere in the world.

9. Make sure that our expenses are equal to the money we make, so we can _____ this month.

10. James is always trying to _____. When he forgot to send the report last week, he said that it was my fault for not mailing it on time, but that wasn't true.

11. Everything breaks so easily these days. I think the manufacturers really _____ when they make products now.

12. As soon as the manager _____, I can get started on the new project.

PRACTICE

■ EXERCISE 1

A. 🎧 *Listen to the conversations with everyday idioms (you heard them in the Check Yourself exercise on page 29). Then look at the statements and check (✓) True or False.*

		True	False
1.	The woman recommends talking about personal issues at parties.	☐	☐
2.	The woman doesn't want to hear the man's opinion.	☐	☐
3.	The man did not agree to help the woman's brother.	☐	☐
4.	Tim was able to talk to Marsha about her trip.	☐	☐
5.	The woman contacted Maggie yesterday.	☐	☐
6.	The man accidentally used the wrong word.	☐	☐
7.	The man feels bad about not communicating with Jean.	☐	☐
8.	Margaret convinced Dana to loan the car to her.	☐	☐
9.	The man thinks that what the woman said about Ellen is unkind.	☐	☐
10.	The man wishes the woman would have waited to speak.	☐	☐

B. *Match the statements to the responses.*

_____ 1. I really dislike **making small talk.**

_____ 2. Thanks for **staying in touch with** me.

_____ 3. Hey, could you slow down for a minute? I **can't get a word in edgewise.**

_____ 4. Please stop **putting words in my mouth.**

_____ 5. Yes, you **hit the nail on the head!**

_____ 6. I couldn't **get in touch with** Amy this morning.

_____ 7. Wow! You just **took the words out of my mouth**.

_____ 8. I tried **to talk Kim into** buying a new car.

a. Thanks. It feels good to know that I got it exactly right.

b. Did you try to call her or email her?

c. Me, too. I'd rather talk about something more interesting and important.

d. I guess we were thinking the same thing.

e. Sorry, I didn't realize I wasn't giving you a chance to talk.

f. Really? Were you able to persuade her to do it?

g. It's been fun calling you while you're traveling so I can hear about all the places you've been.

h. Oh, sorry. I didn't mean to answer for you.

■ EXERCISE 2

🎧 *Listen to the conversations with workplace idioms. Then read the statements and circle the correct information.*

1. People in (*some / all*) of the departments will lose their jobs.

2. Now is (*the right time / a bad time*) for Meg to apply for the job at David's company.

3. The restaurant is having a (*successful / disappointing*) opening. The menu isn't (*exciting / boring*).

4. Liz (*has / doesn't have*) enough money to take another trip.

5. They (*will / won't*) have enough money to operate their business.

6. Martin is suggesting a way for Carla to spend (*the same amount / much more*) of the money that the company gave her.

7. The chairman (*agreed to / was against*) Maria's request for a new assistant.

8. Tina (*can start / must stop*) designing the advertisement.

9. Debbie did a (*great / poor*) job on the report. She said her co-workers were (*responsible / not involved*).

10. Gina's daughter is (*involved / not involved*) in a lot of different activities.

■ EXERCISE 3

Read the interview with Fred Douglas, the CEO (chief executive officer) of a new publishing company. Match the interviewer's questions to the CEO's responses. Use the context to help you.

Interviewer

_____ 1. I understand that you take an innovative approach to publishing, Mr. Douglas. Can you talk about that a little, please?

_____ 2. I read that you started your own company because the publisher you worked for didn't like your ideas. Is that right?

_____ 3. What made you decide that it was the best time to publish these kinds of books?

_____ 4. Is it true that you are still involved in every part of the process, from helping to find writers to reviewing the books?

_____ 5. And your company has been quite successful right from the beginning, hasn't it?

_____ 6. So, you'll start selling overseas, including most of Europe, soon?

Fred Douglas (CEO of Lifetime Publishing)

a. Well, we did **get off to a flying start.**

b. Yes, it's my personality. I do like to **have my fingers in every pie.**

c. Actually, we are already selling our books in France, Germany, Italy . . . **across the board** in the European market.

d. It's true that my previous employer **threw cold water on** my ideas.

e. Yes, we try to **think outside the box** and only publish books about people who have really interesting lives.

f. Our marketing surveys indicated that a majority of people like this kind of book, so we had to **strike while the iron was hot.**

■ EXERCISE 4

A. Work with a partner. One of you is Student A and the other is Student B. Read the situations. Then follow the instructions to write short conversations using the correct idioms for the phrases in bold.

1. **Student A**
   Imagine you and Student B are discussing ways to make the apartment you share more attractive. Explain that you would like to **say something important** but that you are unhappy because Student B **isn't giving you a chance to talk**. Then give two ideas for making your apartment look nicer.

   Student B
   Thank Student A for **saying exactly the right thing**. Tell Student A to **say what** he or she **thinks directly and honestly** in the future.

2. **Student A**
   Imagine that you are Student B's boss. Congratulate Student B for **finding a creative solution to a problem** that will help your company **make money and be successful**.

   Student B
   Tell Student A that you're glad he or she **gave you permission to go ahead** and search for a solution. Mention that **now is the perfect time** to use the solution to solve the problem.

3. **Student A**
   Imagine that Student B is your friend. Tell Student B that you understand why he or she has **not communicated for a long time** with an old friend with whom he or she has had trouble in the past. Encourage Student B **to start communicating again with** his or her old friend.

   Student B
   Tell Student A that he or she **has persuaded you** to talk to your old friend even though you didn't want to at first. Express regret that you didn't **continue communicating with** your old friend.

4. **Student A**
   Imagine that Student B is your coworker. Ask Student B why he or she **discouraged** you from planning to open a new coffee shop. Tell Student B that you are sure you can make this business **a success from the beginning**.

   Student B
   Explain to Student A that many coffee shops in the area have recently been **losing money** and that there is no way to make a profit unless he or she **wants to reduce services in order to save money**.

B. Practice your conversations with your partner. Then choose one to perform for the class.

PUT IT TOGETHER

Student Council Meeting

A student council is a group of students, usually chosen by other students, that represents the interests of all students at a college or university. A student council generally presents plans and ideas to a university board, which is made up of officials from the school's administration. The council may also have the power to approve or disapprove of university plans.

In this section, you will listen to a group of student council members discussing improvements to their university's on-campus food service. Most colleges and universities have cafés, cafeterias, or large dining halls on campus for their students.

■ EXERCISE 1

A. 🎧 *Listen to a student council meeting. The students are discussing the food services on their university campus. Take notes to help you answer questions about the meeting later.*

B. *Circle the correct answers to the questions. Use your notes from Exercise A to help you.*

1. Which campus food services does the student council president say need to be improved?

   a. most of the dining halls

   b. the Rise and Shine Café and Mickey's Coffee House

   c. all of the food services on campus

2. Does Susan agree with James's point about the kind of food the dining halls serve?

   a. Yes, she agrees that the food is uninteresting and too expensive.

   b. No, she would like to see more chicken dishes offered for variety.

   c. Yes, she also wants a better food service to open around the corner.

3. What is James's response to the president's comments on vegetarian food?

   a. He's upset that the president stopped him from speaking.

   b. He was thinking exactly the same thing.

   c. He disagrees with the idea of offering more salad.

4. How does Lisa feel about the discussion?

   a. She agrees with everything that has been said.

   b. She feels that people are making excuses for the food services.

   c. She feels that she hasn't had a chance to speak.

5. Why does the president use the term "slip of the tongue"?

   a. He didn't remember someone's name.

   b. He forgot to say something.

   c. He said something that was confusing.

6. What does the president think about Lisa's idea?

   a. He doesn't understand what she said.

   b. He wants to talk about it more after the meeting.

   c. He thinks it's very original and creative.

7. How does the president think the university board might respond to their ideas?

   a. He is sure that they will like the students' ideas.

   b. He's worried that they might not allow the changes.

   c. He is not sure whether they will want to talk with him.

8. What does the president hope they can do after he contacts the university board?

   a. persuade the board to make the changes they've discussed

   b. discuss the changes that the board would like to make

   c. continue to communicate with the board after the changes are made

■ EXERCISE 2

A. *Read the email. Look at the phrases in parentheses ( ). Then complete the email with the idioms from the box that mean the same thing.*

be in the red	get in touch with [someone]
be out of touch with [someone]	have [someone's] fingers in every pie
break even	strike while the iron is hot

From: Jay Brown, manager, Hemel Food Service, Inc.
To: Nicholas Johnson, CEO, Hemel Food Service, Inc.
Subject: Establishing a food service on the XYZ University campus
📎 **Attachment:** (58KB) Student Council suggestions

Hello Nic,

I'm writing to let you know about an exciting new business possibility. Until recently, I had (not communicated for a long time) (1) _____ my old friend, Peter. However, when he (contacted) (2) _____ me, I found out that he is a member of the XYZ University Board. Peter is the type of guy who (gets involved in a lot of different things) (3) _____ on campus. He told me that the Student Council at the university is very unhappy with their current food service. So he suggested that we should arrange a meeting with the board to promote our food service. This is exactly the right time (to take advantage of the situation) (4) _____. I understand that the current food services (are losing money) (5) _____ because the students have decided to start eating at other places off-campus. The Student Council has suggested a lot of changes, and some of them might be expensive in the beginning, but we probably would (not lose more money than we would spend) (6) _____.

I'm attaching a detailed document. Please let me know if you are interested in this opportunity.
Regards, Jay

B. 🎧 *Listen to the phone message. Take notes on a separate piece of paper. Then work with a partner to circle the correct answers to the questions. Use your notes to help you.*

1. Why is Nicholas Johnson calling Jay Brown?

   a. to tell Jay that it will not be possible to meet with the university board

   b. to thank Jay for making a presentation to the student council

   c. to give Jay permission to start setting up a food service

2. What does Nicholas suggest that Jay do in order to have a successful beginning?

   a. ask the student council to attend the presentation to the university board

   b. accept the student council's invitation to attend its presentation

   c. have a meeting with him before he contacts the university

3. What does Nicholas worry might happen if Jay doesn't follow his suggestion?

   a. The university board might decide not to offer Hemel Food Service the business.

   b. The university board and the student council might blame each other.

   c. Jay will not clearly understand how to approach the student council with a business plan.

4. What is the purpose of Nicholas's request for a financial plan?

   a. He indicates that it will help solve problems with the current food service.

   b. He says that the university requires it four months in advance.

   c. He needs it to make sure that the company will make money.

■ EXERCISE 3

Work in groups. Imagine that you are a member of the student council at your school. Come up with a plan to make an improvement to your school. Choose one of the following topics and create a role play.

food services	classrooms	technology
transportation	class trips	clubs or sports
library	class schedules	your own ideas

Before you begin your role play:

- With your group, choose six idioms from this unit and list them on a piece of paper. Check to make sure that everyone remembers the meanings of the idioms.

During your role play:

- Keep the list of idioms in the middle of the table so all group members can see it. Your group should try to use all of the idioms at least once during the role play.

- Try to use both everyday and workplace idioms.

Example

 OK. Let's get started. Do I have the green light to share some ideas about ...?

■ EXERCISE 4

Idioms are everywhere! Work in a group to find 10 idioms from advertisements in magazines or websites, in song titles, on clothing and posters, and so on. Look up the definition for each idiom, write it down, and then create a sentence using it. Present your idioms to the class and have them try to guess the meanings. Then give the class the definitions of the idioms along with your sample sentences.

Comprehension Focus

Unit Warm Up

A. *Imagine the diagram below represents a lecture. Label the parts of the diagram as follows:*

> Main Idea
>
> Supporting Ideas
>
> Details

B. *Discuss the diagram with a partner. Explain your answers from Exercise A.*

C. *Discuss these statements with the class. Which of these do you think is a main idea? Which is a supporting sentence? Which is a detail?*

- For one thing, they introduced musical elements that had never been heard in pop songs.
- The Beatles were one of the most innovative musical groups of the twentieth century.
- For example, they played musical instruments from India in some of their songs, such as "Norwegian Wood."

SKILL PRESENTATION

When we listen, we are interested in different types of information. *How* we listen depends on the type of information we are listening for. We may need to understand only the main points of a conversation or a lecture, or we may need to summarize the important points of a meeting, a presentation, or a business discussion. Sometimes we need to listen for supporting ideas such as examples and reasons. Other times, we need to focus our attention on very specific details, such as dates or times.

In this unit you will learn the differences between these different types of information and how you can effectively listen for them in English.

The Topic

The *topic* is the subject of a lecture. If someone asks you, "What was that lecture about?" you would probably answer by stating the topic. A topic is usually expressed as a noun, a noun phrase, or an *-ing* phrase or a noun clause. The *topic* is often used as the *title* (name) of a lecture.

Examples

> *why seawater is salty*
>
> *dangerous snakes*
>
> *choosing the best university*

Signal Phrases: Topic

The speaker usually introduces the topic in the introduction to a lecture. There are various ways a speaker might introduce a topic. Listen for these topic signal phrases:

Today, I want to focus on ….

Tonight, we'll be discussing …

This afternoon, we'll be talking about …

In this lecture, we'll concentrate on …

Two Important Points about Topics

- A topic should not be too general.

Suppose you hear a lecture about the nutritional value of eating fruit. You would not say that the topic was "eating healthy" because that topic is too general. The topic "eating healthy" would probably include information about other healthy foods—vegetables, for example—that are *not* mentioned in the lecture. A better way to state the topic is "why eating fruit is healthy" or "why fruit is good for you."

• A topic should not be too specific.

Imagine you hear a lecture about different ways to do research for a term paper. You would not say that the topic is "using the library" if the speaker also talks about ways to do research outside the library (on the Internet, for example). A more appropriate way to express the topic would be "term paper research techniques" or "how to do research for a term paper."

☑ Check Yourself

🎧 *Listen to the introductions to two lectures. Circle the answers to the questions.*

Introduction 1

1. What is the topic of this lecture?

   a. growing a garden

   b. raising tomatoes

   c. protecting tomato plants from insects

2. This lecture will probably include information about _____.

   a. planting tomato seeds

   b. cooking with tomatoes

   c. the history of the tomato

3. This lecture will probably *not* include information about _____.

   a. insects that eat tomato plants

   b. growing carrots

   c. the best time to plant tomatoes

Introduction 2

1. What is the topic of this lecture?

   a. the costs of building a high-speed train network

   b. the future of the travel industry

   c. the benefits of a high-speed train system

2. This lecture will probably include information about _____.

   a. the environmental effects of building high-speed trains

   b. how to make reservations for high-speed train travel

   c. how much it would cost to build a high-speed train system

3. This lecture will probably *not* include information about _____.

   a. the negative effects of high-speed trains

   b. the effects of high-speed trains on the economy

   c. how high-speed trains could make life easier

Main Idea and Purpose

The *main idea* of a lecture is a statement about the topic. It may also include information about the speaker's opinion or the main point that the speaker wants to make. If someone asks you, "What did the speaker say about that topic?" or "What does the speaker think about the topic?" you would probably explain by stating the main idea. A main idea is usually expressed as a complete sentence.

Examples

> *Although there are many dangerous snakes, most are harmless and useful.*
>
> *There are five important steps to choosing the best university.*

The *purpose* of a talk or a lecture is the speaker's reason for speaking. If someone asks you, "Why did the speaker give that lecture?" you would respond by stating the speaker's purpose. For example, a speaker may be providing information or explaining a topic. On the other hand, the speaker may be trying to persuade people to do something, to buy something, or to change their minds about something. The purpose of a lecture is usually expressed as an infinitive phrase (*to* + verb + noun phrase).

Examples

> *to show that most snakes are not only harmless but also useful creatures*
>
> *to help high school students choose the best possible university*

☑ Check Yourself

A. *State whether each of the following is the topic, the main idea, or the purpose of a lecture. Write T (topic), M (main idea), or P (purpose).*

_____ a. Mammals and reptiles are different in many important ways.

_____ b. mammals and reptiles

_____ c. to define mammals and reptiles and contrast these two types of animals

B. 🎧 *Listen. Write your answers to the questions.*

1. What is the *topic* of this short lecture?

   _____

2. What is the *main idea* of this lecture?

   _____

3. What is the speaker's *purpose*?

   _____

Supporting Ideas

A lecture or a presentation can really have only one main idea. However, the speaker may express several or many important ideas. In a lecture that makes an argument or expresses an opinion, these important points are called *supporting ideas*. That's because these ideas usually support the speaker's opinion or develop the main point of the argument.

Signal Words and Phrases: Supporting Ideas

Speakers use a variety of signal words and phrases to introduce supporting ideas at different points in a lecture. These words and phrases can be used to introduce the first important idea, add additional important ideas, and conclude with a final important idea.

First Supporting Idea	Additional Important Ideas	Last Important Idea
First, …	Next, …	Finally, …
First of all, …	In addition, …	Last, …
For one thing, …	For another thing, …	One last thing …
The first point I'd like to make is …	Another point I'd like to make is …	A final point …

☑ Check Yourself

A. 🎧 *Listen to the beginning of this lecture and read along. Circle the main idea and underline the two supporting ideas.*

This afternoon, I want to talk about the proposal for a new local sales tax, which you will soon be voting on. I know that many people favor this proposed tax increase, and I agree that we need to change the current tax policy. However, there are several reasons why I oppose this particular proposal. First of all, this new tax will cost consumers—That's you—a lot of money! For another thing, this tax will hurt small businesses.

B. *Write the two signal phrases the speaker used to introduce supporting ideas.*

_____   _____

Details

Although it is certainly important to understand the important points of a lecture, it is also often necessary to understand detailed information. In the same way that supporting ideas can be used to strengthen main ideas, specific details can be used to strengthen supporting ideas. Details can include specific information, such as specific examples, reasons, or personal experiences.

Certain words and phrases can introduce specific details.

Signal Words and Phrases: Details

Examples	Reasons	Personal experiences
For example, …	That's because …	Here's an example from personal experience:
Let me give you an example:	Because of …	In my experience …
For instance, …	For one reason, …	Speaking from my own experience, …
	Why? Because …	

☑ **Check Yourself**

A. 🎧 *Listen and read along. Underline the details the speaker gives.*

This afternoon, I want to talk about the proposal for a new local sales tax, which you will soon be voting on. I know that many people favor this proposed tax increase, and I agree that we need to change the current tax policy. However, there are several reasons why I oppose this particular proposal. First of all, this new tax will cost consumers—That's you—a lot of money! For instance, if you buy a new car for $20,000, you'll pay $200 more for sales tax. For another thing, this tax will hurt small businesses. Why? Because if sales taxes are high, people shop less.

B. *Write the two signal phrases the speaker uses to introduce details.*

_____   _____

> **Note**
> Not all lectures follow this pattern (main idea/supporting ideas/details) but many do, especially academic lectures.
>
> Identifying main ideas and supporting ideas and understanding details are important skills for standardized English tests such as the TOEFL©, TOEIC©, and IELTS©. These tests include questions that ask you to listen and identify the topic, purpose, or main idea of a lecture and answer questions about supporting ideas and specific details.

PRACTICE

■ EXERCISE 1

🎧 **Topic, Main Idea, Purpose** *Listen to the introductions to three lectures. Circle the answers to the questions.*

1. The topic of Lecture 1 will be _____.

   a. the launch of Voyager II

   b. visiting the outer planets

   c. the story of the Golden Record

(continued)

2. The main idea of Lecture 2 will be: _____.

   a. Mountain gorillas can be very dangerous.

   b. *Gorillas in the Mist* was a remarkable movie in several ways.

   c. Mountain gorillas continue to face dangers.

3. The purpose of Lecture 3 will be to _____.

   a. provide evidence that continental drift actually happens

   b. attack the theory of continental drift

   c. explain how the theory of continental drift was first proposed

■ EXERCISE 2

A. 🎧 **Main Idea** *Listen. Write the main idea of the lecture in your own words.*

_____

_____

B. 🎧 **Supporting Ideas** *Listen again. Check two of the supporting ideas the speaker mentions.*

☐ a. Lighting with coal-gas was less expensive than lighting with electric lights.

☐ b. Electric lights were brighter than coal-gas lights.

☐ c. Coal-gas lights were more dangerous than electric lights.

☐ d. Most people preferred to use coal.

C. Details *Write your answers to the questions. Then compare your answers with a partner.*

1. According to the speaker, what did electric light allow people to do?

_____

2. What are two dangers the speaker mentions of using coal-gas lights?

_____

■ EXERCISE 3

Vitamin D

For many years, nutritionists have known that vitamin D is important to human health in a number of ways. Recently, however, scientists have learned some new information about this important vitamin. Try taking notes as you listen.

A. Vocabulary Preview *Match the words to their definitions. Use a dictionary if necessary.*
Then use the words to complete the sentences below.

_____ 1. deficiency

_____ 2. immune system

_____ 3. building material

_____ 4. supplement (*noun*)

_____ 5. salmon

_____ 6. sunscreen

_____ 7. block

_____ 8. harmful

_____ 9. boost

_____ 10. inadequate

a. the parts of the body that prevent or fight disease

b. an amount that is added to make something complete

c. not enough; less than is required

d. a lotion or liquid that is put on the skin to prevent damage from the sun

e. dangerous; causing damage

f. a lack or shortage of something

g. a type of fish

h. to increase; to raise

i. wood, stone, and brick used to construct houses

j. to stop; to prevent something from reaching

11. In areas where there are a lot of trees, wood is often the most common _____ for houses.

12. Whenever I eat at a seafood restaurant, I order _____. It's my favorite.

13. Some race-car drivers use a special kind of fuel to _____ the power of their engines and increase the speed of their cars.

14. Before you go to the beach, put some _____ on. You don't want to get a sunburn.

15. Eating citrus fruits like oranges and lemons can prevent a vitamin C _____.

16. He must have a strong _____, because he almost never gets sick.

17. There hasn't been any rain for six months, so the city may have an _____ supply of water this summer.

18. The trees outside her window _____ most of the afternoon sunlight.

19. Smoking is _____ to your health.

20. Everyone needs iron. If you don't get enough, you may need to take iron _____.

B. 🎧 **Main ideas and supporting ideas** *Listen to the lecture. Follow the instructions for each question.*

1. Check (✔) the important supporting ideas from the lecture. (Do *not* check details or incorrect information.)

   ☐ a. It was recently discovered how important vitamin D is to human health.

   ☐ b. The government suggests that people take 5,000 IU of vitamin D every day.

   ☐ c. Most people do not get enough vitamin D from foods or one-a-day vitamins.

   ☐ d. Salmon is rich in vitamin D.

   ☐ e. Sunlight is an important source of vitamin D.

   ☐ f. It's important to use lots of sunscreen every time you go out in the sun.

   ☐ g. It is recommended that people take vitamin D supplements and spend some time in the sun.

   ☐ h. It's easy to take too much vitamin D.

2. Circle the main purpose of the lecture.

   a. to discuss the effects of vitamins on health

   b. to explain the dangers of taking too much vitamin D

   c. to show how vitamin D prevents serious diseases

   d. to argue that many people don't get enough vitamin D

C. 🎧 **Supporting Ideas and Details** *Listen again. Then work with a partner. Write the letters of two supporting ideas from the box under each main idea on page 51.*

> Details
>
> a. Many people spend most of their days doing indoor activities.
>
> b. People should supplement their diet with vitamin D pills.
>
> c. Most vitamin supplements contain only 400 IU, which is not enough.
>
> d. Vitamin D increases bone strength.
>
> e. People use sunscreen to block the sun's harmful rays.
>
> f. Vitamin D boosts the immune system and helps prevent diseases.
>
> g. Everyone should spend some time in the sun.
>
> h. Fish such as salmon contain vitamin D, but nutritionists say they don't contain enough for the body's needs.

I. Vitamin D: important for health

_____   _____

II. Diet and one-a-day vitamin pills: inadequate sources of vitamin D

_____   _____

III. Sunshine: for most people, not as good a source as in the past

_____   _____

IV. Recommendations

_____   _____

D. 🎧 **Details** *Listen again. Circle the correct answers.*

1. One scientist says that _____ people around the world don't get enough vitamin D.

   a. several million   b. more than a billion

2. Vitamin D is important to bone health because it _____.

   a. is the basic building material of bones   b. helps the body absorb calcium

3. Foods such as _____ and salmon have quite a bit of vitamin D.

   a. meat   b. milk

4. A serving of salmon has _____ IU of vitamin D.

   a. 150 to 250   b. 450 to 750

5. Most one-a-day vitamin pills have _____ recommended by the U.S. government.

   a. the amount of vitamin D that is   b. less vitamin D than is

6. Vitamin D is sometimes called the _____ vitamin.

   a. sunshine   b. salmon

7. The speaker says that spending 20 minutes in the sun to increase your vitamin D is probably _____.

   a. safe   b. unnecessary

8. Vitamin D from sunlight is _____.

   a. not as useful as vitamin D from food   b. never toxic

E. *Work in groups. Discuss these questions.*

1. According to the information in the lecture, do you think you get enough vitamin D in your diet? Why or why not?

2. What kinds of food do you eat to be healthy? What kinds of foods do you avoid?

3. Do you think it's difficult to eat healthy foods? Why or why not?

■ EXERCISE 4

A. *Choose one of these topics and prepare a one-minute mini-lecture. Write notes for your lecture below.*

Why people should have pets	Tips for finding a good job
Ways to learn English vocabulary	Cell phone manners
Interesting places to travel	Why people should/shouldn't watch TV

Topic:

Introduction (Introduce the main idea):

Supporting Idea 1:

Details:

Supporting Idea 2:

Details:

Conclusion:

B. *Work with a partner. Practice giving your mini-lectures. Remember to use signal words and phrases for introducing the topic, main idea, and supporting ideas and details.*

C. *Join another pair. Take turns presenting your mini-lectures.*

Applying Your Skills For additional practice listening for main ideas, supporting ideas, and details, turn to Part 2, Unit 5, pages 85–86.

Making Inferences

Unit Warm Up

Work with a partner. Look at the pictures. What can you guess about who the people are and about what they are doing, thinking or feeling? What do you think is happening or going to happen in each situation? Make at least two guesses about each picture.

SKILL PRESENTATION

Listening "Between the Lines"

An inference is a conclusion or a judgement. Sometimes we have some information about a topic or a situation, but we don't have enough direct information to know that something is definitely true. So we make a guess based on the information that we do have. This is an inference.

Making an inference is really a two-part process. It involves combining new information with the prior knowledge you have from your past experience or education.

New Information	+	Prior knowledge	→	Inference

Sometimes we use the idiom "read between the lines" to describe this process when we are reading. You can learn to "listen between the lines" too.

We make inferences constantly in our daily lives. We use all five of our senses to gather information and then make "educated" guesses about that information. For example, if we smell fresh coffee, we infer that someone nearby is making a pot of coffee, even if we don't see anyone making coffee. Of course, our inferences aren't always correct.

We often use inferences to understand:

- the topic of a conversation or a talk
- the relationship between speakers
- the speakers' opinions, attitudes, and feelings
- the speakers' real meaning when they speak indirectly

☑ Check Yourself

🎧 *Listen to two conversations. Write your answers to the questions. Then write any words or phrases that helped you make the inference.*

Conversation 1

1. What can you infer about the southwestern part of the state?

   _____

   Words and phrases: _____

2. What can you infer about the grandfather's farm?

   _____

   Words and phrases: _____

Conversation 2

1. How does the man probably feel about broccoli?

   _____

   Words and phrases: _____

2. How does the man probably feel about cherry pie?

   _____

   Words and phrases: _____

Making Inferences from Tone of Voice

We often use our tone of voice to express the way we feel about something. If you learn how to listen for tone of voice, you can get hints about the real meaning of what someone says. We can often infer a lot of information from a surprised, angry, or happy tone of voice, even if the actual words the speaker uses have a different meaning. (See Part 1, Unit 2, for more information about tone of voice and intonation.)

🎧 *Listen to the conversations. Write your answers to the questions.*

Conversation 1

1. The boy really wants to _____.

    a. stay   b. go

2. At the end of the conversation, the boy feels _____.

    a. angry   b. sad

Conversation 2

1. The man means that _____.

    a. he doesn't really want a   b. this type of motorcycle
       motorcycle like this one   is very expensive

2. The man is probably _____ buy a motorcycle like this one.

    a. going to   b. not going to

Conversation 3

1. We can infer that Dean Metzger _____.

    a. often gives long speeches   b. is an interesting speaker

2. The woman probably _____.

    a. has heard Dean Metzger speak before   b. doesn't know who Dean Metzger is

PRACTICE

■ EXERCISE 1

🎧 *Listen to the short conversations. Write your answers to the questions.*

1. What does the man think about the box?

    _____

2. How does Jody feel about the Harry Potter books?

    _____

3. What does the man mean by his response?

    _____

4. How does the woman feel about Robert's work on the project?

    _____

5. What probably happened to the woman?

    _____

(continued)

6. What do we learn from the conversation about Room 18?

_____

7. What are the people probably looking at?

_____

8. What is the man's opinion of the Blue Dolphin Restaurant?

_____

9. How does the man feel about the change of schedule?

_____

10. What can you infer about Andy?

_____

11. What will the woman probably do on her trip this weekend?

_____

12. What do we learn about Mill Street?

_____

■ **EXERCISE 2**

A. 👂 *Listen to the TV cooking show. Circle the answers to the questions.*

1. The host suggests that her show is for people who have _____.
   a. a lot of cooking experience   b. very busy lives

2. The host of this show believes that many of her viewers _____.
   a. are not familiar with gazpacho   b. prefer cold soups to hot ones

3. We can infer that some of the viewers of this show are _____.
   a. young children   b. university students

4. The host indicates that gazpacho is _____.
   a. easier to prepare than canned soup   b. healthier than canned soup

5. We can infer that gazpacho _____.
   a. does not have to be cooked   b. must first be heated, then cooled

6. We can infer that, during the commercial break, the speaker will cut up _____.
   a. bread   b. vegetables

B. 👂 *Listen to the weather report. Circle the answers to the questions.*

1. We can infer that the weather report is being given during _____.
   a. mid-winter   b. autumn

2. We can infer that the snow in the northeastern suburbs _____.
   a. will stop soon   b. was heavier than in other parts of the city

3. We learn that the snowstorm that occurred two years earlier _____.

    a. caused fewer problems than this storm   b. brought more snow than this storm

4. The weather reporter will probably spend the weekend _____.

    a. working at the television station   b. traveling in the countryside

C. 🎧 ***Listen to the talk about giant sea spiders.***
Circle the answers to the questions.

1. We can infer from this talk that the speaker is a _____.

    a. diver   b. scientist

2. The speaker indicates that some sea spiders have _____.

    a. more than eight legs   b. fewer than eight legs

3. The speaker mentions a *dinner plate* _____.

    a. because some people   b. to give listeners an idea of
       eat sea spiders   the size of sea spiders

4. The speaker implies that the discovery of deep-water fish with large eyes _____.

    a. was a great surprise   b. indicates that there is
       to scientists   light at the sea bottom

■ **EXERCISE 3**

Laughter Club, India

Laughter Clubs

Did you know that laughing is good for your health? Around the world, people are joining laughter clubs in order to take advantage of this healthy habit.

A. Vocabulary Preview *Match the words to their definitions. Use a dictionary if necessary. Then use the words to complete the sentences below.*

_____ 1. yoga

_____ 2. hearty

_____ 3. exhausted

_____ 4. prescribe

_____ 5. pretend

_____ 6. relieve

a. strong and vigorous

b. very tired

c. a style of exercise and stretching that enables a person to get control over the mind and body

d. imagine; act as though something were real even if it is not

e. recommend medicine or treatment

f. make something better; remove pain

7. Doctors don't usually _____ drugs for the common cold. They usually just tell patients to rest.

8. I'm not used to running long distances. After I ran 10 kilometers, I felt _____.

9. When I first visited my wife's family, they all hugged me and gave me a _____ welcome. They really made me feel at home.

10. My niece Donna likes to _____ that she is a princess.

11. Annabelle is taking _____ lessons to get in shape and to reduce stress.

12. Many people take aspirin to _____ the pain of a headache.

> **Useful Terms**
> **oxygen:** the gas found in the air that people breathe
> **blood pressure:** the force with which blood travels through the body

B. 🎧 *Listen to the talk. In the left column, check (✓) true or false for each statement. (You will complete the right column in Exercise C.)*

(Exercise B)

(Exercise C)

True	False		Inference	Direct Statement
☐	☐	1. There are 65 Laughter Clubs in each of the 100 countries.	☐	☐
☐	☐	2. Norman Cousins was the first person to popularize Laughter Yoga.	☐	☐
☐	☐	3. Dr. Kataria believes that laughter cannot only cure disease but also prevent it.	☐	☐
☐	☐	4. At first, the people in the original Laughter Club found the jokes funny.	☐	☐

(Exercise B)			(Exercise C)	
True	False		Inference	Direct Statement
☐	☐	5. Dr. Kataria believed that laughing was more important than the jokes.	☐	☐
☐	☐	6. The "cocktail laugh" includes the "silent laugh" and the "dancing laugh."	☐	☐
☐	☐	7. Laughter Yoga can be very tiring.	☐	☐
☐	☐	8. Dr. Kataria believes that it is as useful to pretend to laugh as it is to actually laugh.	☐	☐
☐	☐	9. During the first part of a Laughing Yoga session, people are pretending to laugh, but by the end, they are actually laughing.	☐	☐
☐	☐	10. Dr. Kataria thinks that Laughter Yoga has many positive effects and a few negative ones.	☐	☐

C. 🎧 **Check your answers to Exercise A with your teacher. Then listen again. For the <u>true statements</u> in Exercise A, check (✓) whether the information is an inference or a direct statement in the lecture.**

■ EXERCISE 4

A. **Work with a partner. Choose one of the situations below and write a conversation. Use your tone of voice to express different attitudes or opinions. Practice your conversation.**

At the hair salon	At a friend's wedding
At a job interview	At an amusement park
After an English test	At the library
At the beach	At a sports event

Example

....

A: OK, sir. I'm finished with your haircut. Let me get a mirror. Do you like it?

B: Uh, yes. It's very nice. Thank you.

A: You're welcome! That will be fifty dollars, please.

B: Fifty dollars? Really?

B. **Join another pair. Take turns presenting your conversations.**

Applying Your Skills For additional practice making inferences, turn to Part 2, Unit 6, pages 90–91.

Unit Warm Up

A. Work with a partner. Discuss these questions.

1. What is the difference between a *fact* and an *opinion*?

2. Read this quotation about facts and opinions. What do you think it means?

"Every man has a right to his opinion, but no man has a right to be wrong in his facts."

Bernard Baruch

B. 🎧 **Listen to six statements about the picture. Are they facts or opinions? Check (✓) your answers.**

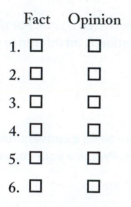

Fact   Opinion

1. ☐ ☐
2. ☐ ☐
3. ☐ ☐
4. ☐ ☐
5. ☐ ☐
6. ☐ ☐

C. 🎧 **Listen again. Which words or phrases tell you whether each statement is a fact or an opinion? Tell the class.**

SKILL PRESENTATION

Many of the lectures and conversations that you hear contain a mixture of facts and opinions. In typical university lectures, for example, professors often cite facts and express their own opinions. They also often give facts and opinions offered by experts in the field. It is important to be able to distinguish facts and opinions so that you can evaluate and understand the information that you hear.

Statements of Fact

A statement of *fact* is an expression of something that is true, that actually happened, or that can be verified in an objective way. In other words, you can prove in some way that the statement is true.

A fact can be verified (checked) with reference books such as encyclopedias, atlases, or the book, *Guinness World Records*. Facts can also be confirmed with statistical documents or by scientific experiments, experts in the field, personal observations, and many other sources. Many people go to the Internet to confirm facts. However, remember that the "facts" that you read on the Internet or in any of these other sources are not always "facts." It's useful to check several reliable sources to be sure.

Signal Words and Phrases: Facts

The following phrases are often used to introduce facts:

In fact, …	There's no doubt that …
As a matter of fact, …	Experts/scientists have confirmed that …
We know that …	Statistics show that …
As we know, …	It's certain that …
It's well known that …	In reality, …
It's true that …	According to …
It's a fact that …	

Examples

It's a fact that the earth circles the sun.

It's well known that the Pacific is the largest ocean.

We know that Leonardo da Vinci was not only a painter but also a scientist and an inventor.

It's a fact that Brazil produces more coffee than any other country.

Statements of Opinion

A statement of *opinion* expresses a feeling, an attitude, a judgement, or a conclusion about something. You'll hear opinions expressed every day in advertisements, political speeches, formal lectures and debates, as well as in informal conversations. You can agree or disagree with an opinion, and you can find information to support an opinion or to oppose an opinion, but you can never *prove* that an opinion is right or wrong or true or false.

Example

Read these two statements:

There are twenty-four students in my psychology class.

I think there are too many students in my psychology class.

The first statement is a fact. It can be verified by checking the teacher's class list or by counting the students in the class.

The second statement is an opinion. The expression "too many" is subjective. The speaker may think twenty-four students is too many, but other people may think it is just the right number or not enough.

Signal Words and Phrases: Opinions

There are many signal words and phrases that can indicate that a speaker is giving an opinion:

I feel / think / believe …	I would argue that …
I find …	In my opinion, …
I bet …	It's my opinion that …
To me, …	Apparently, …
I imagine …	…. should / shouldn't …
Personally, …	… probably …
I'm sure you'll agree that …	

Examples

Personally, I think these fees are too high.

It's my opinion that students shouldn't be scheduled for classes before 8 AM.

I'm sure you'll agree that everyone needs to take a vacation at least once a year.

I bet Julia will be late again.

I believe that the grade Professor Thompson gave me was unfair.

According to my brother, this restaurant has the best sandwiches in town.

> **Note**
> Some phrases can actually signal both opinions and facts.
>
> **Examples**
>
> *A: "Joan says that Prince Edward Island is the smallest province in Canada."*
>
> *B: "As a matter of fact, she's right." = FACT (The information can be checked.)*
>
> *A: "Joan says that British Columbia is the most beautiful province in Canada."*
>
> *B: "As a matter of fact, she's right!" = OPINION (There is no way to prove the information.)*

☑ Check Yourself

🎧 *Listen. Is the statement a fact, an opinion, or does it contain both a fact and an opinion? Check (✓) your answer.*

	Fact	Opinion	Both
1.	☐	☐	☐
2.	☐	☐	☐
3.	☐	☐	☐
4.	☐	☐	☐
5.	☐	☐	☐
6.	☐	☐	☐
7.	☐	☐	☐
8.	☐	☐	☐
9.	☐	☐	☐
10.	☐	☐	☐

Objective and Subjective Adjectives

Certain adjectives are often used to express facts. We call these *objective* adjectives because they describe qualities that can be measured and verified. Other adjectives, called *subjective* adjectives, describe qualities that have a personal meaning. For example, *heavy* is an objective adjective, because we can weigh something and find out if it is heavy or not. *Beautiful* is a subjective adjective because different people have different opinions about beauty.

☑ Check Yourself

Are these objective or subjective adjectives? Write O for objective or S for subjective.

_____ cold		_____ silly	
_____ clever		_____ fast	
_____ friendly		_____ expensive	
_____ tall		_____ early	
_____ wonderful		_____ high	
_____ long		_____ unattractive	
_____ blue		_____ safe	
_____ boring		_____ young	

PRACTICE

■ EXERCISE 1

🎧 *Listen to the conversation. Write your answers to the questions.*

1. What is Matthew's opinion of New Orleans?

   _____

   _____

2. How does Amy feel about New Orleans?

   _____

   _____

3. What did Matthew think about the Nightshade restaurant?

   _____

   _____

4. What is Amy's opinion of the Nightshade restaurant?

   _____

   _____

5. What does Matthew think about Amy's opinion?

   _____

   _____

■ EXERCISE 2

A. 🎧 *Read the statements about the tropical fruit, durian. Then listen to the lecture. Mark the statements **F** for fact or **O** for opinion.*

_____ 1. Durian is one of the most fascinating tropical foods.

_____ 2. Durians are grown in Malaysia, Indonesia, and Thailand.

_____ 3. People often call durian the "king of fruits."

_____ 4. Alfred Russell Wallace wrote about durians in the eighteenth century.

_____ 5. Durians taste like almond-flavored dessert.

_____ 6. The taste of durians is unusual but enjoyable.

_____ 7. You can smell durian even before it has been opened up.

_____ 8. The smell of durians is unpleasant and disgusting.

_____ 9. Many hotels do not allow guests to eat durian in their rooms.

B. 🎧 *Read the statements about the web site* **Wikipedia.** *Then listen to the announcement. Mark the statements F (fact) or O (opinion).*

_____ 1. Most of the students in the teacher's class are already familiar with *Wikipedia*.

_____ 2. *Wikipedia* articles are written by the site's users.

_____ 3. *Wikipedia* is published in about forty-five languages.

_____ 4. The word *wiki* comes from the Hawaiian language.

_____ 5. Articles in *Wikipedia* sometimes contain incorrect information.

_____ 6. The problem of errors in *Wikipedia* has been exaggerated.

_____ 7. It's fine to use *Wikipedia* to get preliminary information for a research paper.

_____ 8. Students must read at least five journal articles before they write their papers.

_____ 9. Copying information directly from *Wikipedia* is cheating.

_____ 10. Students who cheat may have to leave the university.

Language Learning Challenges

Every language is different, but some languages may be more difficult to learn than others. What factors make a language easier or more difficult to learn?

■ EXERCISE 3

A. Vocabulary Preview *Match the words to their definitions. Use a dictionary if necessary.*

_____ 1. factor

_____ 2. tone

_____ 3. linguist

_____ 4. diplomat

_____ 5. gender

_____ 6. turnip

_____ 7. slice the pie

_____ 8. motivation

_____ 9. master (verb)

a. a term used to describe words in some languages that are considered masculine (male), feminine (female), or neuter (neither masculine nor feminine)

b. someone, such as an ambassador, who represents his or her government to another country

c. to learn completely; to become skillful in some field

d. a condition or influence that helps cause a result

e. a large, round root vegetable

f. divide something into parts

g. a person who studies languages

h. desire or determination to do or to achieve something

i. the pitch or change in pitch of a word in some spoken languages that distinguishes that word from words that otherwise sound the same; a tone may be high, low, rising (low to high), falling (high to low), etc.

B. Predict *Look at the speaker's notes on the board. What do you think this lecture will be about?*

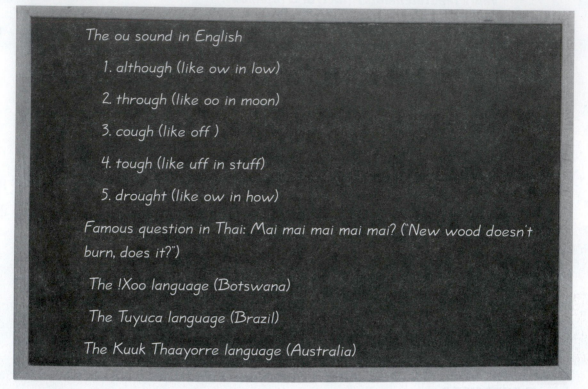

The ou sound in English

1. although (like ow in low)

2. through (like oo in moon)

3. cough (like off)

4. tough (like uff in stuff)

5. drought (like ow in how)

Famous question in Thai: Mai mai mai mai mai? (`New wood doesn't burn, does it?")

The !Xoo language (Botswana)

The Tuyuca language (Brazil)

The Kuuk Thaayorre language (Australia)

C. 🎧 *Listen to the lecture. Circle the signal phrases the speaker uses.*

1. Now, (*I think / it's certain*) that Spanish is one of the easier languages to pronounce because each letter in Spanish is pronounced only one way; if you can read a word, you can pronounce it.

2. I (*believe / know*) that it's mainly the pronunciation—and of course the spelling—of English that makes it a challenging language to learn.

3. In southern Africa, there are "click" languages which contain sounds that—well, (*actually / to me*), these clicks sound like someone trying to get a horse to move.

4. As (*is well known / you'll no doubt agree*), in languages like Chinese, Vietnamese, and Thai, words may have several different tones that can change the meaning of a word.

5. (*In fact / It's thought that*), in Thai, the word *mai* can have five different tones with five different meanings.

6. (*There's no doubt / I believe*) that gender is a problem, especially for people who grew up speaking a language with natural gender, such as English.

7. Now, many people (*think, and I would agree / know, and I wouldn't argue*), that some languages are difficult because—well, because speakers of that language have a different way of looking at reality.

8. Now (*certainly / personally*), I think it's impossible to name the most difficult language.

9. (*In my opinion / As a matter of fact*), a lot depends on the learner.

10. Then too, (*it's a fact / I find*) that some people are just better language learners than others.

D. *Do the statements in Exercise C express facts or opinions? Check (✓) your answers.*

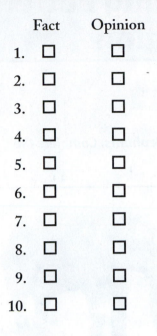

Fact   Opinion

1. ☐   ☐
2. ☐   ☐
3. ☐   ☐
4. ☐   ☐
5. ☐   ☐
6. ☐   ☐
7. ☐   ☐
8. ☐   ☐
9. ☐   ☐
10. ☐   ☐

■ EXERCISE 4

Work with a partner. Follow these instructions:

1. Choose one of the statements below to discuss. One of you agrees with the statement and the other disagrees with the statement. Decide who will take which role.

2. Work individually to prepare a one-minute mini-lecture expressing your opinion. Your mini-lecture should contain at least three opinions and three facts related to the topic. Use signal phrases from the Skill Presentation.

3. Take turns presenting your mini-lectures.

   - Standardized English tests such as the TOEFL© and TOEIC© are a good way to decide who is admitted to a university or who gets a job.

   - Governments should promote tourism because it is a non-polluting, "clean" industry that brings in a lot of money.

   - It should be legal to copy computer software, movies, and music.

   - Schools should give grades of *Pass* or *Fail* instead of giving letter grades such as A+, B-, C, etc.

   - One of the biggest problems the world faces is global warming.

   - Health care should be free for everyone.

> **Applying Your Skills** For additional practice distinguishing facts and opinions, turn to Part 2, Unit 6, page 91.

Understanding Patterns of Organization

Unit Warm Up

A. 🎧 *Listen to part of a lecture about African and Asian elephants. Complete the information below the pictures.*

African Elephant	**Asian**
Height: Up to _____ meters tall	**Height:** Up to _____ meters tall
Weight: Up to _____ kilograms	**Weight:** Up to _____ kilograms
Tusks: _____	**Tusks:** _____ or _____
Ears: _____, shaped like _____	**Ears:** _____, shaped like _____

B. *Work with a partner. Take turns giving the talk in your own words. Use the information below the pictures. Use comparative adjectives (taller, smaller, etc.).*

SKILL PRESENTATION

The lecture in the Unit Warm Up makes a comparison between two different types of elephants. Comparison is one common pattern for organizing a lecture. A speaker often organizes a formal lecture according to a particular pattern of organization. These patterns can show the way a speaker thinks about a topic and can indicate the speaker's goal or purpose. For example, the speaker might organize a lecture in a certain way to compare two concepts, to explain how to do something, or to define a concept.

Listening for patterns of organization in lectures makes it easier to understand and remember the information you hear.

Pattern of Organization	Explanation	Sample Introductions
Comparison/Contrast	The speaker shows how two things or two concepts are the same (comparison) and/or different (contrast).	*Today I want to discuss how A and B are similar …* *We are going to discuss how A differs from B in a number of ways …*
Cause/Effect	The speaker shows how one event or condition causes another (cause) or explains the result of some event (effect).	*In this lecture, I want to explain the reasons for …* *Let's begin by talking about what happened as a result of …*
Definition	The speaker explains what a term or a concept really means.	*Now I want to define what we mean by _____.* *What do we mean when we say ____?*
Chronological Order	The speaker lists a sequence of events in the order in which they happened.	*The topic of today's lecture is the history of …* *The first important event was …*
Process	The speaker explains the steps that are required to do something.	*There are five steps you must take to complete this task.* *The first thing you need to do is …*

☑ Check Yourself

🎧 *Listen to the introductions to five different lectures. Decide which of these patterns of organization the lecture will probably follow. Write the letter of the pattern.*

_____ 1.   a. Comparison/Contrast

_____ 2.   b. Cause/Effect

_____ 3.   c. Definition

_____ 4.   d. Chronological Order

_____ 5.   e. Process

The Comparison/Contrast Pattern

Comparison/contrast is one of the most common ways to organize a lecture or part of a lecture. A lecture that follows this pattern of organization usually covers two or more items that have some points in common. For example, a lecture comparing two universities might compare the number of students, the dates the universities were founded, the programs offered, and so on.

There are two main patterns for showing similarities and differences: the *block style* and the *point-by-point style*.

Block Style

In the block style of a comparison/contrast lecture, the speaker first lists several points about one item and then moves on to present the same points related to the second item.

🎧 **Listen to a short lecture about Earth and Venus organized in the block style. Follow along with the outline.**

Earth and Venus
I. Earth
A. Earth's size
B. Earth's temperatures
C. Earth's atmosphere
II. Venus
A. Venus's size
B. Venus's temperatures
C. Venus's atmosphere

Point-by-Point Style

In the point-by-point style, the speaker presents one point or feature of the first item (Earth's size) and then compares the same feature of another item (Venus's size). Next, the speaker presents a second point related to the first item (Earth's temperatures), followed by the same point about the second item (Venus's temperatures). The pattern continues until all points have been compared. The point-by-point style is especially useful if a lecture compares many points.

🎧 **Listen to the same lecture about Earth and Venus organized in the point-by-point style. Follow along with the outline.**

Earth and Venus	
I. Size	**III. Atmosphere**
A. Earth's size	A. Earth's atmosphere
B. Venus's size	B. Venus's atmosphere
II. Temperatures	
A. Earth's temperatures	
B. Venus's temperatures	

Signal Words and Phrases: Comparison/Contrast Pattern

The following words and phrases are commonly used in comparison/contrast lectures:

Comparison	Contrast
Likewise, …	However,…
Similarly, …	On the other hand,…
A is similar to B in that …	While A ___, B ___ …
Like A, B is …	Although A ___, B ___ …
Both A and B …	A differs from B in that ….
A is like B in that …	Unlike A, B …
A is the same (size/shape/color, etc.) as B …	A is (*bigger*, *nicer*, *older*, etc.) than B.

☑ Check Yourself

A. 🎧 *Listen to a lecture comparing two cities, Tokyo and Bangkok. Look at the outline below. Is the lecture organized in the block style or the point-by-point style?*

B. 🎧 *Listen to the lecture. Complete the information in the outline.*

Tokyo and Bangkok

I. Importance
  A. Tokyo: capital city, center of business and industry
  B. Bangkok: _____

II. Climate
  A. Tokyo: _____
  B. Bangkok: hot year round

III. Population
  A. Tokyo: _____
  B. Bangkok: about 9 million

IV. Sights
  A. Tokyo: Imperial Palace, _____
  B. Bangkok: thousands of temples (Temple of Dawn), _____

C. *Change the organization of this lecture from the point-by-point style to the block style. Use the blank chart to write an outline of the lecture in block style.*

I. _____	II. _____
A. _____	A. _____
B. _____	B. _____
C. _____	C. _____
D. _____	D. _____

D. 🎧 *Listen again. Write the words or phrases you hear that signal the comparison/contrast pattern. The first one is done as an example.*

While

The Cause/Effect Pattern

The *cause/effect* pattern is also a very common way to organize lectures or parts of lectures. Various patterns are possible.

One Cause-One Effect

The speaker may present only one cause and one effect.

🎧 *Look at the diagram as you listen to the introduction to a lecture about viruses.*

CAUSE: viruses ⟶ **EFFECT:** many diseases in humans

One Cause-Several Effects

The speaker may present one cause for several effects.

🎧 *Look at the diagram as you listen to another introduction.*

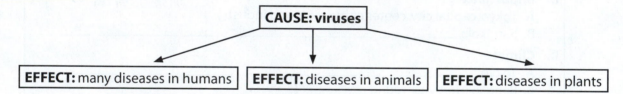

CAUSE: viruses

EFFECT: many diseases in humans **EFFECT:** diseases in animals **EFFECT:** diseases in plants

Several Causes-One Effect

The speaker may present two or more causes for one effect.

🎧 *Look at the diagram as you listen to the conversation.*

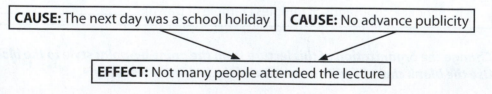

CAUSE: The next day was a school holiday **CAUSE:** No advance publicity

EFFECT: Not many people attended the lecture

Chain Reaction

The speaker may discuss a chain reaction: one cause creates an effect, which causes another effect, and so on.

🎧 *Look at the diagram as you listen to the conversation.*

> **CAUSE:** Supply of gasoline goes down.
>
> ↓
>
> **EFFECT/CAUSE:** Demand for gasoline goes up.
>
> ↓
>
> **EFFECT/CAUSE:** Price for gasoline goes up.
>
> ↓
>
> **EFFECT:** Demand for fuel-efficient vehicles goes up

Signal Words and Phrases: Cause/Effect Pattern

The following words and phrases are commonly used when presenting cause/effect lectures:

A leads to B	As a result …	because	because of
A causes B	Consequently,…	since	due to
A results in B	Therefore ….	so	on account of
B is caused by A	Thus, …		
B is an effect of A	If … then ...		
B is a consequence of A			
B is a result of A			
One reason for A is B			

☑ Check Yourself

A. 🎧 *Listen to a short lecture about dinosaurs. Look at the chart in Exercise B. Which pattern do you think the lecture will follow?*

    a. one cause for several effects

    b. several causes for one effect

    c. a chain reaction of causes and effects

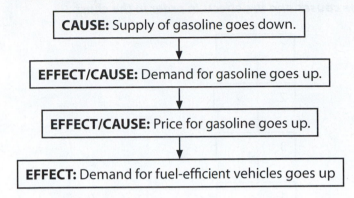

B. 🎧 *Read the list of causes and effects below. Then listen to the lecture. Write the letters of the causes and the effects in order in the chart.*

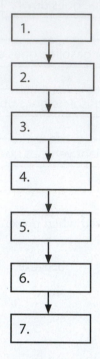

1.

2.

3.

4.

5.

6.

7.

a. The skies turned black and temperatures fell.

b. Plant-eating dinosaurs died because there weren't enough plants to eat; meat eating dinosaurs died because their food source disappeared. They could no longer hunt the plant-eating dinosaurs.

c. This caused forest fires and threw rock dust into the air. Winds blew the smoke and dust around the world.

d. The dust blocked the sun's light and heat.

e. An asteroid hit the earth near present-day Mexico.

f. The age of the mammals began.

g. Cold weather destroyed most of the plant life around the world.

C. 🎧 *Listen to the lecture again. Write the words you hear that signal the cause/effect pattern.*

_____

_____

Definition

A *definition* is the meaning of a word or concept. Sometimes an entire lecture may involve the definition of one word or concept, but usually a definition is part of a longer lecture. Speakers often provide definitions when a word or concept is difficult or unfamiliar, or when a familiar word or concept is used in an unusual way. (See Part 3, Unit 4, for more on definition patterns.)

Signal Words and Phrases: Definition

The following phrases and sentences signal the definition pattern:

Today, I am going to define the concept of _____.　_____ is defined as …

The definition of _____ is …　_____ consists of …

By _____, I mean …　_____ is composed of …

We can define _____ by …　_____ is made up of …

What do we mean by _____?

In other words, …

Chronological Order

If a lecture follows *chronological order*, it is organized according to the time at which a series of events happened. Chronological order is often used to discuss a news story, a historical event, or events in a person's life.

Signal Words and Phrases: Chronological Order

Certain words and phrases, especially sequence adverbs and time expressions, are often used to signal chronological order.

Sequence adverbs	Time expressions	
First, …	In the nineteenth century, …	On Saturday ….
Then, …	In 1974, …	On the next day, …
Next, …	In May, …	Later that week, …
After that,…	Two months later, …	That morning …
Afterwards, …	Later that month, …	Later in the day, …
Following that, …	On October 7, …	At 9:30, …
Subsequently, …		
Later, …		

☑ Check Yourself

A. 🎧 *Read the list of events. Then listen to a short lecture about the International Space Station (ISS). Number the events in the correct order from 1 to 9.*

_____ Work on the ISS in Earth orbit began.

_____ The shuttle *Columbia* had a terrible accident.

_____ Astronauts began living on the station permanently.

_____ The space station stopped all operations.

_____ The first private citizen to go into space visited the station.

_____ The shuttles began to fly again.

(continued)

_____ The number of astronauts on the station was reduced.

_____ Planning for the ISS began.

_____ Work on the ISS was completed.

B. 🎧 *Listen again. Write the word that is defined in the lecture and its definition.*

Word: _____   Definition: _____

C. 🎧 *Listen again. Write the words and phrases that signal chronological order.*

_____

Process

Process is a pattern of organization that involves giving directions or suggestions. A process lecture tells you how to do something or explains how something is made or how something happens.

Signal Words and Phrases: Process

Many of the signals for a process lecture are the same sequence adverbs as those used for chronological order.

First, …	After that, …	The next step is to …	Finally, …
Then, …	Next, …	Following that, …	

☑ Check Yourself

A. 🎧 *Read the list of steps. Then listen to a short lecture about getting a driver's license. Number the steps in the correct order from 1 to 8.*

_____ Take a written test and a vision test.

_____ Get a driver's manual and study it.

_____ Practice your driving skills.

_____ Take a driving test.

_____ Get a temporary license.

_____ Receive a permanent license in the mail.

_____ Get a driving permit.

_____ Pass the driving test.

B. 🎧 *Listen again. Write the word that is defined in the lecture and its definition.*

Word: _____   Definition: _____

C. 🎧 *Listen again. Write the words and phrases that signal a process.*

_____

PRACTICE

■ EXERCISE 1

A. 🎧 *Listen to three short lectures. Check (✓) the patterns of organization used in each lecture. (There may be more than one pattern for each.) Listen for signal words and phrases to help you.*

Lecture 1: Bees in Danger

- ☐ Comparison/Contrast
- ☐ Cause/Effect
- ☐ Definition
- ☐ Chronological Order
- ☐ Process

Lecture 2: Fighting Stage Fright

- ☐ Comparison/Contrast
- ☐ Cause/Effect
- ☐ Definition
- ☐ Chronological Order
- ☐ Process

Lecture 3: The History of Sudoku

- ☐ Comparison/Contrast
- ☐ Cause/Effect
- ☐ Definition
- ☐ Chronological Order
- ☐ Process

Sudoku

2	5			9	7	3		6
		7	3			1		2
	3	1	4		5	8		
	6		8				2	7
	2	4		1			3	8
	8		9			6	1	
3		5			4			1
		6			9	7		
	7		5	1		4		3

B. 🎧 *Listen again. Write the signal words and phrases you hear in each lecture.*

Lecture 1: _____

_____

Lecture 2: _____

_____

Lecture 3: _____

_____

🎧 *Listen again to the lectures in Exercise 1. Circle the answers to the questions.*

Lecture 1: Bees in Danger

1. The speaker defines CCD as _____.

   a. a disease caused by a virus

   b. a condition with an unknown cause

2. The speaker thinks that the *least* likely cause of the disappearance of bees is _____.

   a. a chemical used to kill harmful insects

   b. radiation from cell phones and cell phone towers

3. If bees disappear from the world, _____ will not be affected.

   a. fruit and nuts

   b. rice and wheat

4. To help solve this problem, the speaker suggests that people _____.

   a. give money

   b. grow flowers

Lecture 2: Fighting Stage Fright

1. The speaker defines stage fright as a fear of _____.

   a. actors

   b. performing

2. The speaker says that too much stage fright can lead to _____.

   a. physical sickness

   b. a poor performance

3. The speaker gives a definition of _____.

   a. visualization

   b. deep breathing

4. The speaker suggests that actors think of audience members as _____.

   a. friends and family

   b. vegetables

Lecture 3: The History of Sudoku

1. The speaker says that Sudoku is different from other puzzles and games because it was not developed _____.

   a. by one person

   b. in one country

2. The first person to invent a puzzle similar to Sudoku was from _____.

   a. Japan

   b. Switzerland

3. Sudoku was given its name by _____

   a. Maki Kaji

   b. Howard Garns

4. One of Wayne Gould's main contributions to Sudoku was to develop a _____.

   a. new set of rules for completing puzzles

   b. computer program to create puzzles

■ **EXERCISE 3**

Two Types of Typing

You probably know how to type using a computer keyboard, but do you know how the keyboard was developed or why the letters are arranged that way? The answer is an interesting story.

A. Vocabulary Preview *Match the words to their definitions. Use a dictionary if necessary. Then use the words to complete the sentences below.*

_____ 1. businesslike	a. a choice; one possibility of two or more
_____ 2. row	b. to disappear
_____ 3. get stuck	c. having a strong feeling or inclination about a matter
_____ 4. prejudiced	d. professional; acceptable in a professional environment
_____ 5. vanish	e. to become unable to move
_____ 6. option	f. a horizontal line

7. The new office manager sent us a memo saying that she wanted everyone to dress in a more _____ fashion. She said no blue jeans or t-shirts.

8. Don't put the paper into the printer that way! It will _____, and you'll have to spend a long time getting it out.

9. I can't find the file I was working on last week. It just seemed to _____!

10. When I graduated from university, I had the _____ of taking a job with a big company or going to graduate school.

11. My father doesn't like his new phone, but he's _____. He doesn't like any kind of technology.

12. When I go to the movies, I don't like to sit in the first _____ of seats. It hurts my neck to look up at the screen from there.

B. 🎧 *You will hear a lecture about two types of keyboards: the Dvorak and the QWERTY. The speaker uses the following patterns of organization in the lecture. Read the list. Then listen to the lecture. Number the patterns of organization in order from 1 to 6.*

QWERTY Keyboard

DVORAK Keyboard

_____ **Comparison/Contrast:** The speaker contrasts the QWERTY and the Dvorak keyboards.

_____ **Process:** The speaker explains how to try Dvorak.

_____ **Cause/Effect:** The speaker explains why businesses preferred typewriting to handwriting.

_____ **Cause/Effect:** The speaker explains why Dvorak never became the standard keyboard system.

_____ **Cause/Effect:** The speaker gives another reason why the QWERTY system was first used.

_____ **Chronological order:** The speaker explains how the typewriter was invented and adopted by businesses.

C. 🎧 *Listen again. Mark the statements* **T** *for True or* **F** *for False.*

_____ 1. One reason why businesses began to use typewriters was that typed documents looked more businesslike than documents written by hand.

_____ 2. The speaker suggests that the arrangement of letters on keyboards depends on the language of the users.

_____ 3. The speaker suggests that the arrangement of letters on a QWERTY keyboard has changed several times since it was introduced

_____ 4. The main reason the QWERTY arrangement was used was to increase typists' speed.

_____ 5. The speaker says that the QWERTY arrangement may have been a type of advertising.

_____ 6. The QWERTY keyboard was probably designed for the comfort of right-handed people.

_____ 7. The Dvorak system is actually older than the QWERTY system.

_____ 8. Dvorak typists are typically faster and more accurate than QWERTY typists.

_____ 9. The fingers of a Dvorak typist cover more distance than the fingers of a QWERTY typist.

_____ 10. The speaker suggests that the 1950s' government study comparing QWERTY and Dvorak was not a fair study.

_____ 11. The speaker suggests buying a Dvorak keyboard.

_____ 12. The speaker indicates that he thinks the Dvorak system should replace the QWERTY system.

D. 🎧 *Listen again. Use signal words and phrases to complete the sentences from the lecture.*

1. The typewriter was invented in 1866. _____, typewriters began to be used by businesses. _____, almost all business letters were being typed, not written by hand. _____? Well, _____ you can type a business letter faster than you can write it by hand. _____ is that a typed letter is also easier to read, and typed letters just look more businesslike.

2. Now, look at a standard keyboard. _____ does it have such a strange arrangement of letters?

3. _____ the QWERTY keyboard was invented, basically: to slow typists down.

4. In the 1930's, _____ years of study, a professor at the University of Washington invented another keyboard arrangement called the Dvorak keyboard— not _____ the arrangement of keys, but _____ that was the inventors name—Doctor August Dvorak.

(continued)

5. For one thing, the Dvorak keyboard is _____.

6. _____ QWERTY, the Dvorak keyboard has the vowels on one side and the most-used consonants on the other.

7. Many people also found that a Dvorak keyboard was _____ than a QWERTY keyboard.

8. If typists work eight hours on a QWERTY keyboard, their fingers travel an average distance of about 29 kilometers a day. Twenty-nine kilometers! No wonder their hands get tired. _____, on a Dvorak keyboard, the typical finger-travel for eight-hours' typing is only about 1.5 kilometers!

9. Why doesn't everyone use Dvorak? There are _____. Dvorak introduced his keyboard during the Great Depression of the 1930s. Businesses did not have enough money to buy new typewriters or re-train typists. Another _____: in the 1950's, a U.S. government study found that QWERTY was more efficient than Dvorak.

10. _____ the experiment was finished, all of his data mysteriously vanished, _____ no one else could check his results.

11. Computer operating systems such as Windows and MAC have an option which allows you to change from one keyboard to another. So _____, you should change your keyboard to Dvorak. Of course, while your keyboard will *work* like a Dvorak keyboard, it will still *look* like a QWERTY keyboard. So _____, order key-covers on-line and _____ use these to cover the keys on your QWERTY keyboard and change to the Dvorak layout. _____, you'll just need to practice, practice, and practice to get used to the Dvorak keyboard.

> **Applying Your Skills** For additional practice with Patterns of Organization, turn to Part 2, Unit 6, page 89 and Unit 7, page 94.

What's Up? McArthur's Universal Corrective Map

Unit Warm Up

In this unit, you will hear about an unusual type of map.

Work with a partner. Discuss these questions.

- Have you ever seen a map like the one below? Where did you see it?

- How is this map different from ordinary maps?

- Look at the title of this unit. What does the phrase "What's up?" usually mean? Why do you think it is used in the title?

- This unit is about McArthur's Universal Corrective Map. What does the word *corrective* mean? Why do you think this is called a *corrective* map?

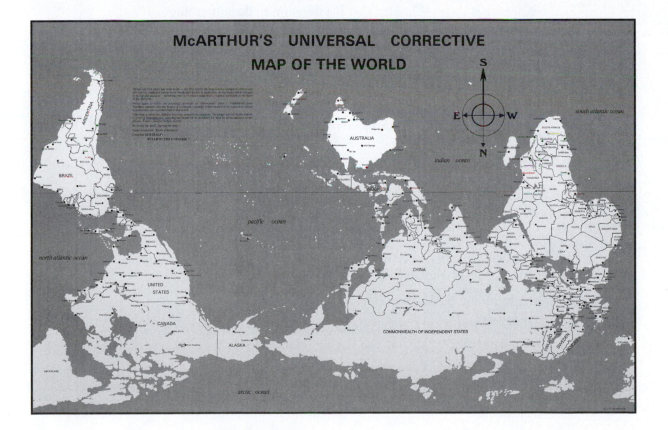

BEFORE YOU LISTEN

Vocabulary Preview *Match the words to their definitions. Use a dictionary if necessary. Then use the words to complete the sentences below.*

_____ 1. standard

_____ 2. wonder

_____ 3. compass

_____ 4. navigate

_____ 5. convention

_____ 6. hemisphere

_____ 7. tease

_____ 8. resolution

_____ 9. inspire

_____ 10. split

a. to make fun of; to joke

b. a custom; a normal way to think about something

c. half a sphere; half a globe

d. to think about; to question

e. an instrument that shows directions (north, south, east, west)

f. to divide; to break into parts

g. ordinary; normal; regular

h. to encourage others to do something, especially something good

i. to find the right direction

j. a decision to do something

11. Australia is in the southern _____ of the earth.

12. I don't know my way around the city. I'll need you to help me _____ while I'm driving.

13. We should buy a _____ before our hiking trip. That way we won't get lost in the woods.

14. Wearing a suit and a necktie is a common _____ in the business world.

15. Do you ever _____ which came first—the chicken or the egg?

16. Yariv is going to become a music teacher at an elementary school. He wants to _____ young children to love music.

17. When Gary finally passed his university exam, he made a _____ to become a doctor someday.

18. I bought a new car last week. It's nothing special, just a _____ economy car.

19. There's only one cookie left, but it's big. Here, let's _____ it into two pieces and share it.

20. We always _____ my sister because she's the shortest person in our family. She doesn't mind; she just laughs.

WHILE YOU LISTEN

First Listening

🎧 **Main Ideas, Supporting Ideas, and Details** *Read the list of statements. Then listen to the lecture. Write **M** for main idea, **S** for supporting idea, or **D** for detail next to each statement.*

_____ 1. After the invention of the magnetic compass, north was always at the top of maps.

_____ 2. McArthur was assigned to draw a map in geography class.

_____ 3. Stuart McArthur began drawing south-up maps as a child and created one of the most famous of the south-up maps.

_____ 4. Some maps, such as Stuart McArthur's, put south at the top of the map.

_____ 5. McArthur's map has inspired other map makers to create south-up maps.

_____ 6. McArthur's map presents an unusual view of the world.

_____ 7. On some standard maps, Australia is in the lower left corner, while on others, it is in the lower right corner.

Second Listening

A. 🎧 **Details** *Listen again. Decide if the sentences are true or false or if there is not enough information to answer. Mark each statement **T** for true, **F** for false, or **?** for not enough information.*

_____ 1. On some ancient maps, south was at the top.

_____ 2. Sailors in China and later in Europe began to use magnetic compasses in the twelfth century.

_____ 3. North has been at the top of most maps for almost a thousand years.

_____ 4. McArthur's geography teacher told him to draw a map of Australia.

_____ 5. When he was twelve, Stuart McArthur failed his geography class.

_____ 6. McArthur went to Japan to study map making.

_____ 7. When McArthur was studying in Japan, students from Australia teased him.

_____ 8. McArthur published his Universal Corrective Map when he was a university student.

_____ 9. McArthur's map was published on New Year's Day in 1979.

_____ 10. McArthur's map is the only south-up map.

_____ 11. McArthur became very rich from the sales of his map.

_____ 12. On McArthur's map, Indonesia, Australia, and New Zealand occupy the most important part of the map.

B. 🎧 **Distinguishing Facts and Opinions** *Listen to two people discussing McArthur's Corrective Map. Who makes these statements? Are they facts or opinions? Check (✓) the correct columns.*

	Man	Woman	Fact	Opinion
1. There is a problem with the map.				
2. North doesn't have to be at the top of a map.				
3. In Australia and other countries, drivers use the left side of the road.				
4. There is no reason why the hands on a clock have to move to the right.				
5. In the Southern Hemisphere, the earth seems to turn in a counter clockwise direction.				
6. If clocks had been invented in Australia, they might turn in the opposite direction.				
7. A clock that turns counter clockwise is a silly idea.				
8. The south-up map is confusing.				
9. The south-up map is better than a standard map.				

AFTER YOU LISTEN

Work in groups. Discuss these questions.

1. If you wanted a world map for your home, would you buy a standard map or a south-up map? Why?

2. What do you think were Stuart McArthur's main reasons for publishing his map?

3. Choose one of these topics and think of a common convention that you think should or could be changed. Tell the class your idea. Then have a class discussion about the advantages and disadvantages.

Traffic/Transportation   Education/School   Food/Cooking

Clothing/Fashion   Business/Work   Home/Living

Aha! Moments

Unit Warm Up

In this unit, you will hear a lecture about some famous people and their "Aha! moments."

Work with a partner. Discuss these questions.

- Describe the photograph at right.
  What do you think the woman is doing?
  Why do you think so?

- What does the expression *Aha!* mean?
  What do you think an *Aha! moment* is?

BEFORE YOU LISTEN

A. 🎧 **Vocabulary Preview** *Listen to the short conversations. Then circle the best definition for the underlined word(s) from the conversation.*

1. <u>Come to</u> means _____.

   a. to enter the mind

   b. to consider briefly

2. An <u>insight</u> is _____.

   a. a clear understanding

   b. a quick look

3. <u>Volume</u> is closest in meaning to _____.

   a. size

   b. shape

4. <u>Displaced</u> means ____.

   a. angered and upset

   b. forced out

5. A <u>compound word</u> is ____.

   a. two words with a single meaning, such as *picture frame* or *book cover*.

   b. a noun and a word that describes it, such as *blue skies* or *new bicycle*.

6. <u>In a flash</u> means ____.

   a. certainly

   b. quickly

7. A <u>surge</u> is a ____.

   a. sudden increase

   b. disappointing result

8. A <u>crown</u> is worn on a king or queen's ____.

   a. head

   b. foot

9. <u>Emphasis</u> means ____.

   a. importance; stress

   b. intention; plan

10. <u>Implementing</u> means ____.

    a. putting into effect; putting into practice

    b. voting for something; being in favor of something

11. An <u>innovation</u> is a ____.

    a. system of communicating

    b. new idea, method, or invention

B. Predict *Are you familiar with any of the names on the board below? What did these people do? What do you think the lecture might say about them?*

> *Karl Bühler early 20th century German psychologist*
> *Sir Isaac Newton 17th century British mathematician*
> *Archimedes ancient Greek mathematician*
> *Peter Drucker 20th & 21st century U.S. business expert*

WHILE YOU LISTEN

First Listening

🎧 **Patterns of Organization** *Read the information in each diagram. Then listen to the lecture. Check (✓) the diagram that best describes the organization of the talk.*

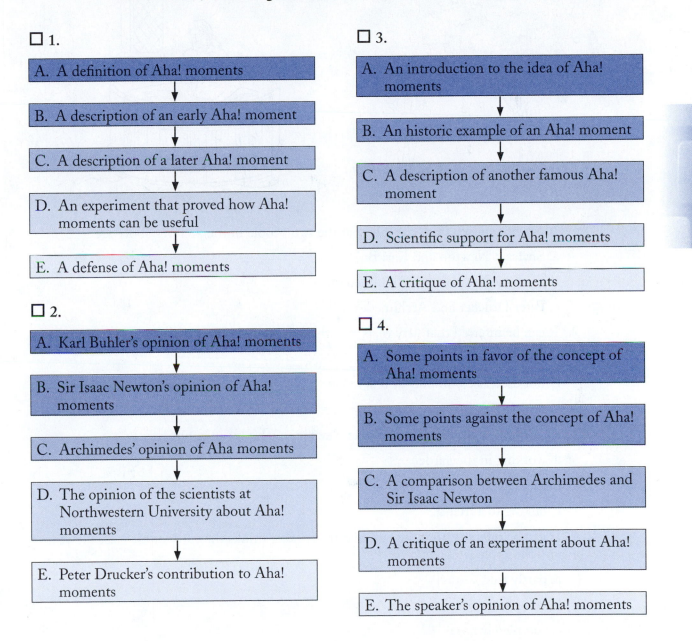

☐ 1.

A. A definition of Aha! moments

↓

B. A description of an early Aha! moment

↓

C. A description of a later Aha! moment

↓

D. An experiment that proved how Aha! moments can be useful

↓

E. A defense of Aha! moments

☐ 2.

A. Karl Buhler's opinion of Aha! moments

↓

B. Sir Isaac Newton's opinion of Aha! moments

↓

C. Archimedes' opinion of Aha moments

↓

D. The opinion of the scientists at Northwestern University about Aha! moments

↓

E. Peter Drucker's contribution to Aha! moments

☐ 3.

A. An introduction to the idea of Aha! moments

↓

B. An historic example of an Aha! moment

↓

C. A description of another famous Aha! moment

↓

D. Scientific support for Aha! moments

↓

E. A critique of Aha! moments

☐ 4.

A. Some points in favor of the concept of Aha! moments

↓

B. Some points against the concept of Aha! moments

↓

C. A comparison between Archimedes and Sir Isaac Newton

↓

D. A critique of an experiment about Aha! moments

↓

E. The speaker's opinion of Aha! moments

Second Listening

A. 🎧 **Details and Inference** *Listen again. Circle the answers to the questions.*

1. It can be inferred from the talk that the two people in the pictures above are _____.

   a. Sir Isaac Newton and Karl Buhler

   b. Sir Isaac Newton and Archimedes

   c. Peter Drucker and Archimedes

2. It can be inferred that fifty years ago, the term *Aha! moment* was _____.

   a. first invented

   b. not used as commonly as it is today

   c. never used

3. According to the story, when Isaac Newton was hit by an apple, he was _____.

   a. working in the garden

   b. drinking tea

   c. talking to a friend

4. It can be inferred from the talk that the speaker thinks the story of Sir Isaac Newton and the apple is _____.

   a. partly true

   b. completely true

   c. completely false

5. Archimedes had to measure _____.

   a. the height of the king of the city

   b. the weight of a stone

   c. the volume of the king's crown

6. Why does the speaker believe that the story about Archimedes may not be true?

   a. The solution that Archimedes discovered would not really work.

   b. The story did not exist until long after Archimedes had died.

   c. Most historians today do not believe that Archimedes was a real person.

7. What did the people in the experiment have to do with the three words?

   a. provide definitions for them and use them in sentences.

   b. find a single word that could be used with all three words.

   c. spell the three words correctly.

8. The speaker implies that the surge of electricity that the scientists observed _____.

   a. was the result of an Aha moment

   b. showed that the people's answers were incorrect

   c. was too small to prove anything for certain

9. Which of the following does Peter Drucker think should get *less* emphasis?

   a. work done before an Aha! moment

   b. the Aha! moment itself

   c. work done after an Aha! moment

B. 🎧 **Distinguishing Facts and Opinions** *Listen again. Are these statements facts or opinions? Check (✓) the answers.*

	Fact	Opinion
1. The term *Aha! moment* was invented by a psychologist.	☐	☐
2. The story of Sir Isaac Newton being hit by an apple is not true.	☐	☐
3. Isaac Newton watched apples fall to the ground.	☐	☐
4. The volume of an irregularly-shaped object can be measured by the amount of water it displaces.	☐	☐
5. The story of Archimedes is not true.	☐	☐
6. There was no electrical surge in the brains of people who solved the problem carefully and slowly.	☐	☐
7. The emphasis on Aha! moments is not useful.	☐	☐
8. A series of small Aha! moments is more useful than one big Aha! moment.	☐	☐
9. Innovation is generally the product of people working together rather than of one individual having a brilliant idea.	☐	☐

AFTER YOU LISTEN

Work in groups. Discuss these questions.

1. Have you ever had an Aha! moment? If so, describe it.

2. Do you think that there is too much emphasis on Aha! moments and not enough on careful research and preparation. Why or why not?

3. Try this word puzzle:

   Here are three groups of words. For each group, try to think of one word that can be used with all three words to form compound words. (Your word can go either before or after the words in the lists.)

   A. pie, pine, sauce

   B. research, clip, bag

   C. fly, dog, key

   Check your answers to the puzzle in number 3 at the bottom of the page. If you were able to solve this problem, did the answers come to you suddenly or as a result of careful work?

4. There are several sites on the Internet where people describe their Aha! moments. Find one of these sites, find a story that interests you, and report about it to the class.

Answers:
A. apple, B. paper, C. house

Unit Warm Up

In this unit, you will hear about a young Dutch woman, Manon Ossevoort, and her amazing trip.

Work with a partner. Discuss these questions.

- What is unusual about this photograph?
- What do you think the woman in the photograph is doing?

BEFORE YOU LISTEN

A. 🎧 **Vocabulary Preview** *Listen to the short conversations. Then circle the best definitions for the underlined word(s) from the conversations.*

1. A <u>posh</u> restaurant is _____.
   a. small and simple
   b. fancy and expensive

2. To travel <u>solo</u> is to travel _____.
   a. alone
   b. quickly

3. An <u>epic journey</u> is a trip that is _____.
   a. long and boring
   b. full of adventure and excitement

4. To <u>turn around</u> is to _____.
   a. stop and go the opposite direction
   b. turn to either the left or right

5. To <u>run into</u> someone is to _____.
   a. make plans to meet a person
   b. meet a person unexpectedly

6. To <u>break down</u> is to _____.
   a. run out of fuel
   b. stop operating

7. To <u>tow</u> a car is to _____.
   a. pull it with another vehicle
   b. steal it

8. A <u>humanitarian organization</u> tries to _____.
   a. improve people's lives
   b. make a profit

9. A <u>stray</u> cat _____.
   a. is smaller than most cats
   b. does not have an owner

10. The <u>tip</u> of South America is the _____ the continent.
    a. water around
    b. very end of

11. A person's <u>belly</u> is his or her _____.
    a. mouth
    b. stomach

WHILE YOU LISTEN

First Listening

🎧 **Patterns of Organization** *Listen to the lecture. Number the events in the correct order from 1 to 8.*

_____ Manon drove through Sudan, Ethiopia, Kenya, and Uganda.

_____ She went to northern Canada for polar training.

_____ Manon and "Biba, the tractor dog" arrived in South Africa.

_____ She took a "test drive" from Amsterdam to Paris.

_____ She found out she couldn't travel to Egypt by boat, so she went back to Genoa, Italy.

_____ She left her home in the Netherlands and began her journey.

_____ She graduated from the university, bought a tractor, and began planning her trip.

_____ Biba had puppies.

Second Listening

A. Topic and Details *Listen again. Circle the answers to the questions.*

1. The speaker's main purpose in giving this talk is to _____.

    a. compare and contrast various types of travel

    b. explain how Manon raises money for her travels

    c. describe Manon's trip and explain how it is amazing

2. Manon's very first destination was _____

    a. Paris

    b. Canada

    c. Athens

3. Manon had to turn around and go to Genoa, Italy, because she _____.

    a. was not able to enter Kosovo

    b. could not travel by ship from Athens

    c. needed to raise more money

4. What problem did Manon encounter in Egypt?

    a. She could not find the right type of fuel for her tractor.

    b. Her tractor broke down and was difficult to repair.

    c. She did not have the right documents to bring her tractor to Egypt.

5. On average, how fast could Manon drive her tractor?

    a. 5 kilometers per hour

    b. 10 kilometers per hour

    c. 20 kilometers per hour

6. How far could Manon travel on one tank of fuel?

    a. 92 kilometers

    b. 140 kilometers

    c. 760 kilometers

(continued)

7. The speaker does *not* mention that Manon receives money from _____.

    a. the sale of her t-shirts on the web site

    b. humanitarian organizations

    c. support from an Italian tractor company

8. The speaker says that Manon's book about her trip _____.

    a. has not been written yet

    b. has been written but not published yet

    c. is not yet available in English

9. Manon traveled to Canada in order to _____.

    a. train for polar travel

    b. finish writing a book

    c. raise some more money

10. When she reaches the South Pole, Manon plans to _____.

    a. build a snowman

    b. put up a flag

    c. leave her tractor

11. From the speaker's final comment, we can assume that, in his opinion, Manon's plan is _____.

    a. remarkable

    b. dangerous

    c. impossible

B. 🎧 **Inference** *Listen to some quotations from Manon Ossevoort's blog about her trip. Check (✓) the information that can be inferred from what you hear.*

☐ 1. The farmers Manon spoke to didn't tell her that her tractor was quite slow.

☐ 2. After separating from her support team, Manon was able to move more quickly.

☐ 3. Manon feels as though the time she has been traveling has passed very quickly.

☐ 4. Manon was able to bring her dog into South Africa without any difficulties.

☐ 5. It is possible for a tractor to burn kerosene in Antarctica.

☐ 6. Manon would probably agree with the idea that "Good things take a long time."

AFTER YOU LISTEN

Work in groups. Discuss these questions.

1. Imagine that you are going to take a slow-speed trip like Manon's. How would you travel? Where would you go? How would you raise money for your trip?

2. Here are some other long-distance trips. Which of these sounds most interesting to you? Why?

   • Karl Busby is attempting to walk around the world. He began at the tip of South America and is currently in Alaska.

   • Stan Cottrell ran the entire length of the Great Wall of China.

   • Kinga Chosczc hitchhiked around the world. (*To hitchhike* is to stand by the side of the road, trying to get rides from drivers.)

   • Becky Simpson is riding a horse from London to Tokyo.

   • Ted Coombs roller-skated across the United States.

   • Ted Simpson traveled 48,000 miles (about 77,000 kilometers) in the Americas, Europe, Asia, Australia, and New Zealand on a motorcycle.

PART

3

Note-Taking Skills

Organizing Your Notes

Unit Warm Up

> As a general rule, the most successful man in life
> is the man who has the best information.
>
> – Benjamin Disraeli

Work with a partner. Read the quotation. Discuss the questions.

- Do you agree with the statement? Why or why not?
- What is the most difficult part of taking notes for you when you are listening for important information in a lecture?

SKILL PRESENTATION

Why Should I Format My Notes?

Learning to take good notes is an essential skill both in school and in the workplace. We often need to take notes on information we hear in lectures and presentations, during phone conversations, or at meetings. One of the first steps in this process is learning how to organize your notes in an appropriate format. This skill is useful because

- you learn to listen more actively and carefully in order to understand the main ideas and details.

- different note-taking formats are useful for different topics and types of information.

- it helps you remember information better.

- organized notes are easier to read, understand, and revise.

How Should I Format My Notes?

Your notes should be organized according to the topic, main idea, supporting ideas, and specific details included in the lecture.

The **topic** is the main subject of the whole lecture. If someone asks you, "What was that lecture about?" you would answer by giving the topic.

The **main idea** is a statement about the topic. It may also include information about the speaker's opinion or the main point the speaker wants to make. The main idea is generally more specific than the topic.

Supporting ideas are ideas that strengthen and expand the main ideas. There may be several important supporting ideas in a talk.

Details are the small, specific ideas that strengthen and add information to both the main ideas and the supporting ideas. Details can be examples, definitions, numbers, dates, names, and so on. They tell you who, what, why, when, where, how, how much, or how many.

See Part 2, Unit 1, for more on topics, main ideas, supporting ideas, and details.

Examples

> Topic: *How to Exercise the Right Way*
>
> Main idea: *If you don't learn to exercise properly, you can hurt yourself.*
>
> Supporting idea: *Lifting weights that are too heavy can damage your muscles.*
>
> Details: *You should start slowly with light weights and then, try heavier weights as your strength increases over time.*

> **General Note-Taking Guidelines**
> - Do not write down every word you hear.
> - Do not use full sentences.
> - Do leave some additional space between the main ideas and in the margins of your notes. You might want to use this space to make later additions or to list specific terms from the lecture or from the course textbook.

There are many styles of formatting for notes. Two of these are the outline format and the column format.

Outline Format

This format can be especially useful for talks, discussions, or lectures that are organized chronologically into a series of events or steps (for example, a history or a process). It also works well when a lecture lists specific features of a topic (for example, "Eight Ways to Stay Healthy").

- Write main ideas on the left.

- Indent a few spaces and then write supporting ideas to the right.

- Continue to indent each time you note a detail or a more specific point.

- Starting with the most general idea and moving to the smallest points, use the system of Roman numerals (I, II = most general), numbers, and letters (a, b = most specific) as shown in the following example:

Example

Topic: Vegetarian and Semi-vegetarian Diets

Introduction

I. Vegetarians

  A. Vegans

    1. No meat, eggs, dairy products

      a. eat vegetables, fruits

      b. eat grains, nuts, seeds, beans   *tofu??*

      c. eat soy products – soy milk ⟶ bean curd

    2. No dietary source of some vitamins

      a. need to take additional vitamins

  B. Lacto-ovo vegetarians ⟶ ("lacto" = dairy, "ovo" = egg)

    1. No meat, eat eggs, dairy products

    2. Diet includes most necessary vitamins

II. Semi-vegetarians

  A. Flexitarians

    1. Eat mostly fruits, vegetables; sometimes meat, poultry, or fish

  B. Pescatarians ⟶ ("pesca" = fish)

    1. Eat mostly plants, sometimes fish

Note

If you prefer, you can simply indent the points without using the numbering or lettering system.

Example

    Vegetarians

       Vegans

          no meat, eggs, dairy products

       lacto-ovo vegetarians ("lacto" = dairy, "ovo" = egg)

          no meat, eat eggs, dairy products

Column Format

This format is especially useful for talks, discussions, or lectures that are organized by cause/effect, comparison/contrast, or problem/solution.

- Write main ideas in a column on the left.
- Write supporting ideas and details on the right.
- Label the columns with specific categories.

Health Benefits of a Vegetarian Diet

Reasons for Diet (Main ideas)	Effects of Diet (Details)
To improve health	- fewer total calories, lower fat–weight loss
	- reduce harmful fats–lower rates of some diseases
	- strengthen body: estimate living 10 years longer
To protect animals	- animals raised for food treated badly–reduces cruelty
	- animals used for testing products suffer– promotes better treatment
To protect the environment	- raising animals for food causes pollution– reduces negative environmental effects
	- raising animals not best use of land: use land for food crops to feed nearly all people on Earth

Remember

Different note-taking formats are useful for different topics and types of information. Practice using both formats and choose the one that is more comfortable for you or that works better for the topic of the lecture.

PRACTICE

■ EXERCISE 1

A. Complete the outline below with the details from the list. Then compare your outline with a partner.

Details:

take a hot bath	play soft music to create a peaceful feeling
30 minutes/day – run, swim, play sports	include more vegetables, fruit, and whole grains
reduce sugar in your diet	think positively
walk to store, don't drive	use stairs instead of elevator
take deep breaths when upset	choose a variety of foods
tips for daily exercise	
reduce stress	

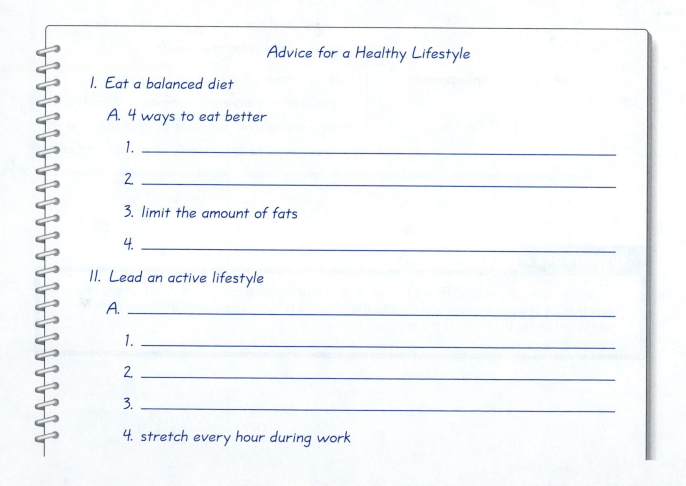

Advice for a Healthy Lifestyle

I. Eat a balanced diet

   A. 4 ways to eat better

      1. _____

      2. _____

      3. limit the amount of fats

      4. _____

II. Lead an active lifestyle

   A. _____

      1. _____

      2. _____

      3. _____

      4. stretch every hour during work

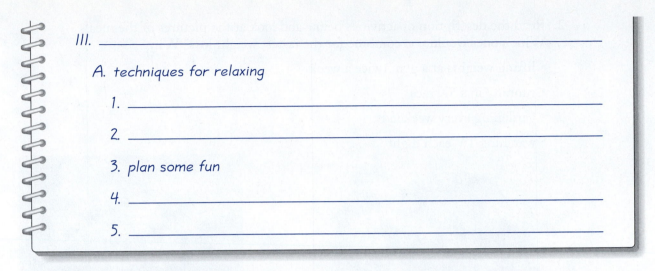

III. _____

    A. techniques for relaxing

       1. _____

       2. _____

       3. plan some fun

       4. _____

       5. _____

B. *Now try the column format. Work with a partner. Use the outline from Exercise A to complete the columns. (Be sure to fill in the topic and the main ideas above each column.)*

Topic: _____		
Eat a balanced diet	_____	_____
A. _____ _____	A. tips for daily exercise	A.
• choose a wide variety of foods	•	•
	•	•
	• walk to store, don't drive	•
•		• take a hot bath
•	•	•
•		

LISTENING TASK

Before You Listen

A. Topic Preview *Work in Pairs. Use the pictures below to discuss these questions. Then share your ideas with the class.*

   1. Based on the pictures of the two meals, which one would you *not* recommend to someone on a diet? Why?

(continued)

2. Read the description of activities below and look at the pictures of the meals. Which ones would you combine for the fastest weight loss? Why?

  • lifting weights at a gym twice a week

  • running in a 5K race

  • gardening every weekend

  • watching TV each night

B. Vocabulary Preview *Read the sentences. Then write each underlined word next to its definition on the next page.*

Did you <u>inherit</u> your brown eyes from your mother or your father?

The price of gasoline increased <u>significantly</u> from nearly $2.00/gallon in 2001 to $4.40/gallon in 2008.

Spending a lot of time in the sun can be <u>potentially</u> harmful if you don't protect your skin.

The fence is starting to fall down. Please <u>reinforce</u> it with some extra pieces of wood.

I'm taking a trip to France, so I need to <u>convert</u> my U.S. dollars into euros.

The brain produces <u>chemicals</u> that act naturally to stop pain in the human body.

The hike was really long and difficult. I had to <u>struggle</u> to get up the mountain.

Polar bears may <u>starve</u> to death if they can't find anything to eat.

One <u>benefit</u> of living on campus is that you have a short walk to class.

There is no change in Jordan's condition. The doctors say he is <u>stable</u>.

Do you <u>retain</u> the information you hear in lectures or do you forget it right away?

Your cell phone is definitely broken. I think it's time to <u>get rid of</u> it and get a new one.

One <u>adaptation</u> of desert mammals is having large ears, which help them release heat in a hot climate.

Joyce's cat is always jumping on the table during dinner. She needs to teach it to <u>behave</u> better.

1. _____ to keep; to store

2. _____ any of the elements or compounds formed from elements

3. _____ an adjustment or change that makes you function better

4. _____ a fight; a great effort

5. _____ to feel extreme hunger and pain or to die due to a lack of food

6. _____ to make stronger

7. _____ support; advantage

8. _____ to change one thing into something else

9. _____ very much; considerably; extremely

10. _____ to remove something that is unwanted

11. _____ to act in a certain way

12. _____ constant; unchanged

13. _____ to receive physical characteristics from parents or ancestors

14. _____ possibly; likely

While You Listen

First Listening

A. 🎧 *Listen to the introduction to a lecture about diet and exercise. Read the following outline as you listen. Do not take notes. Notice how the main ideas and details are outlined.*

> **Useful Terms**
> **calorie:** a unit for measuring the amount of energy food produces
>
> > *Example*
> >
> > *The butter and cream in that recipe adds a large number of calories to your diet.*
>
> **burn calories:** to use up in order to create energy for the body
>
> > *Example*
> >
> > *I'm going to have to run a lot of miles to burn all those calories in the double hamburger I ate.*
>
> **metabolism:** the chemical processes the body uses to change food into energy and use it to support life
>
> > *Example*
> >
> > *Joe can eat as much as he wants and not gain weight because he has a fast metabolism.*

The Human Body Fights Back: Diet and Exercise

Introduction

    A. Weight loss programs/products- do not help lose weight & keep it off

        1. Why? - metabolism inherited from parents

    B. Genes: instructions for how body behaves, include how metabolism works

        1. Metabolism: internal engine powers body, converts food to energy
           (like engine uses gas to power car)

           a. weight gain depends how quickly or slowly metabolism operates

    C. If understand human body's response to dieting, can discover plan to get rid
       of weight

B. 🎧 **Guided Practice** *Listen to the main part of the lecture. Complete the notes.*

I. Problem: Lose weight by dieting, sooner or later (1) _____
weight lost

    A. Reason - body has "set point": weight likes to stay, controls weight to stay
       in range of (2) _____ percent

        1. Adult metabolism - energy made by food balanced by amount energy
           (3)_____ (amount calories eat = amount calories burn in 1 day)

           a. helps weight remain stable long period of time

        2. Sudden & significant increase or decrease (4) _____ – body
           works against change & tries to stay at set point

           a. diet - rapid & large amount weight, chemicals quickly increase = dieter
              hungrier body fights back to defend (5) _____, internal
              struggle = harder to lose weight

B. Reason - body reacts by (6) _____

    1. less food - body "thinks" starved, won't get food long time

    2. when get food, (7) _____ – fewer fat cells burned

        a. metabolism slow down - low amount energy used to produce muscles - reinforces fat storage

        b. process - body created fat-storing adaptation, programmed by genes to (8) _____ for survival when little, no food

C. Check your answers with your teacher.

D. 🎧 **Guided Practice** *Listen to the conclusion of the lecture. Complete the notes.*

II. Solution: (1) _____ & (2) _____

    A. Lose 1 pound fat requires exercise to burn (3) _____

        1. do (4) _____ calories of exercise, cut 300 calories food = (5) _____ a week

        a. if fast walk, 45 minutes, no ice cream or potato chips, can achieve

    B. By exercise, body doesn't think starving, so increase (6) _____

    C. Added benefit - exercise (7) _____, burn more calories than fat

    D. Combine (8) _____ & (9) _____ - best plan for lose weight & not gain back

E. *Work with a partner. Compare your notes from Exercises B and D. Then discuss these questions.*

    1. How are your notes different? How are they similar?

    2. Did you include all the important ideas and details?

Second Listening

🎧 *Follow these instructions:*

1. Listen to part of the lecture and take a new set of notes on a separate piece of paper. Use the column format. Be sure to label each column.

2. Compare your notes with a partner.

3. Use the outline from the First Listening to check your notes. Did you include the same information?

Example

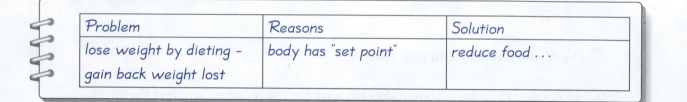

Problem	Reasons	Solution
lose weight by dieting - gain back weight lost	body has "set point"	reduce food ...

Remember

Do not write down every word you hear.
Do not use full sentences.
Do leave some additional space between the main ideas and in the margins of your notes.
Do write the main ideas in the column on the left and the details in the column(s) on the right.

After You Listen

■ EXERCISE 1

Read these statements and check (✓) True or False. Use your notes from the Second Listening to help you.

	True	False
1. The body's metabolism is not programmed by its genes.	☐	☐
2. The metabolism burns food like a car engine uses gasoline.	☐	☐
3. The set point controls body weight, so it stays in a range between 20 and 30 percent.	☐	☐

4. The set point helps to balance the amount of calories eaten with the amount burned in one day. ☐ ☐

5. Losing a lot of weight quickly usually makes you want less food. ☐ ☐

6. During a diet, the body uses food more quickly and more fat is burned. ☐ ☐

7. When the metabolism slows down, less energy is used for making muscles. ☐ ☐

8. Fat is stored by the body for survival when there isn't enough food. ☐ ☐

9. Exercise alone is the best way to lose weight. ☐ ☐

10. Taking a fast, 45-minute walk normally burns 200 calories. ☐ ☐

11. When exercising, the body starts to burn calories more quickly. ☐ ☐

12. Fat burns the same number of calories as muscle. ☐ ☐

■ EXERCISE 2

A. Work in pairs. Discuss these questions.

1. Which note-taking format—outline or columns—did you like the best? Why?

2. Which format was most helpful for answering the true/false questions above? Why?

3. Do you know any another formats for organizing notes? Tell the group.

B. Join another pair. Discuss these questions.

1. What kinds of different diets do you know about? Do you think that any of these diets are effective? Why or why not?

2. Would you like to try a vegetarian or vegan diet? Why or why not?

3. What are some other examples of activities or exercises that could be included every day in an active lifestyle (for example, bicycling to class or work).

4. What techniques do you use to get rid of stress and relax? Why do you think these techniques work?

Omitting Unnecessary Words

Unit Warm Up

A. *Listen to the beginning of a talk about how movie and TV show sound effects are made. Read along with the student's notes. Notice that some words are missing from the notes.*

> How movie sound effects made?
>
> Usually computer software, but some sounds require humans
>
> "Foley artists" = make sound-effects - movies, TV
>
> create sounds = use different objects (paper, plastic bags, pots, pans)

B. *Work with a partner. Discuss the notes in Exercise A. What are some of the missing words? Then listen again.*

C. *Match the sound effects made by a Foley artist to the actions shown in a movie. Then check your answers with your teacher.*

Sound Effects Quiz

Sound effects

_____ 1. pouring water from a glass bottle into soft cotton padding

_____ 2. waving a pair of gloves

_____ 3. blowing through a straw into water

_____ 4. carefully dropping small light bulbs into a glass

_____ 5. rolling a roller skate back and forth on a table

_____ 6. softly hitting a full water bottle

Movie actions

a. filling a glass with ice cubes

b. someone being hit in the stomach

c. drinking water quickly

d. opening/closing a window

e. boiling water

f. bird wings in flight

SKILL PRESENTATION

The average lecturer speaks at a rate of about 120 words per minute. This means a student taking notes during a 50-minute lecture will hear about 6,000 words—so you can understand why it is simply not possible to write down every word. However, there are some essential note-taking strategies you can learn. One key to taking good notes is not only learning what to write down but also what *not* to write down.

I. Focus on content words: Content words contain the important meaning of a sentence. Listen for these key words, which are mostly nouns but sometimes are verbs, adjectives, or adverbs that have important information about the content of the lecture.

II. Omit function words: Function words are the smaller, less important words that do not give a sentence much meaning. In your notes, leave out any words that do not have important meaning for the sentence. The following is a list of the kinds of words you can usually omit:

Forms of the verb *be*:	*am / is / are / was / were*	Relative Pronouns:	*which / that / who / whom*
Auxiliary verbs:	*be / have / do*	Demonstratives:	*this / that / these / those*
Articles:	*a / an / the*	Some prepositions:	*at / from / of*
Personal Pronouns:	*he / she / they / it / them*		

In addition to omitting these words, omit any other unnecessary words or information that doesn't add anything important to your notes.

> **Tips for Taking Short, Clear Notes**
> - Don't write down every word you hear.
> - Do not use full sentences.
> - Use your own words when possible, but try not to change the meaning.
> - Keep descriptions and examples simple and brief.
> - Avoid writing down the speaker's personal stories or comments unless they are important for understanding the topic.

PRACTICE

■ EXERCISE 1

A. *Look at these sentences from a lecture about the history of movie sound effects. Cross out any unnecessary words. Then compare with a partner.*

1. ~~The~~ history of film can't ~~be accurately~~ understood unless ~~it is~~ connected ~~to the~~ major sound practices of each era.

2. Two French brothers, Auguste and Louis Lumiere, are usually credited with the first public screening of film in 1895.

3. The Lumiere brothers' first film screening in Paris consisted of 10 short silent films lasting about 20 minutes.

4. Early films were silent. Actors and actresses had to use exaggerated gestures and facial expressions to communicate emotion.

5. Before the invention of films with sound, known as "talkies," people didn't think sound was necessary to make films more realistic.

6. Silent films, films without sounds, allowed each member of the audience to interpret the action on the screen in his or her own way.

(continued)

7. However, movie theaters that sometimes hired live musicians or pianists to provide background music for the silent films were common.

8. In the early 20th century, they also sometimes employed groups of actors who had carefully practiced matching their spoken words to the images on the screen.

9. If the theater couldn't afford to pay these groups, a single person was brought in to tell the audience the story of what was happening on the screen.

10. Modern movie sound effects first became possible in the late 1800s.

11. They were created by using rather simple technology based on Thomas Edison's invention of the phonograph, an early "talking" machine which could record and play back sounds.

12. It wasn't long until technicians in the 1920s figured out a way to put the phonograph together with film cameras, which allowed the first "talking" movies to be made.

B. Read this excerpt from the same lecture. Underline the most important information.

In New York City on October 6, 1927, the audience heard the first voice spoken in a feature film called *The Jazz Singer*. Talking pictures quickly became very popular in the 1920s, but the introduction of sound had some serious consequences. First, the careers of many actors were affected. Some of their careers ended because their voices didn't match their screen image.

The movie industry was also affected because it had to invest large amounts of money to create the new technologies needed for talking films. The early recording equipment did not always work very well, so they needed creative ways to reproduce certain sounds. To do this, movies borrowed sounds from early radio dramas, which had relied heavily on sound effects during live broadcasts. For example, to make the sound of horses running, two coconuts were knocked together.

Today, there is a large variety of complex sound effects in movies. One category of sound effects is called "designed sounds," which are the sounds of things that don't actually exist in real life, such as a spaceship from another planet landing on Earth. Another category of sound effects is "creature sounds," which are used to create the speech of strange aliens, monsters, or other imaginary animals. Finally, "ambient" sounds that surround you are also produced for background noises: trees blowing in the wind, birds singing, or traffic noises.

C. Look back at the underlined information in Exercise B. Write the important information as notes on a separate piece of paper. Choose the outline or the column format (see Part 3, Unit 1, pages 100–103).

Example
• • • • • • • • •

New York City, October 6, 1927: audience heard 1st voice in
    feature film - The Jazz Singer

I. talking pictures - popular 1920s: introduction sound - serious consequences
    A. careers of many actors affected
        1. ended - voices not match image

LISTENING TASK

Before You Listen

A. 🎧 **Topic Preview** *Listen. Match the sound effects to the correct objects or actions.*

1. ___*i*___   a. human footsteps
2. _____   b. rain
3. _____   c. horse running
4. _____   d. door opening
5. _____   e. wind
6. _____   f. moving train
7. _____   g. birds singing
8. _____   h. door closing
9. _____   i. heartbeat
10. _____   j. car starting

B. *Work in a group. Discuss these questions.*

1. Which sound effects were the most difficult for you to identify? Why?

2. Can you think of any movies in which the sound effects might have been used?

3. How do you think each sound effect is created?

C. Vocabulary Preview *Read each sentence. Then circle the best definition for the underlined word(s).*

1. There were 750,000 people at the concert in the park, an <u>incredible</u> number for an outdoor music event.

    a. amazing   b. estimated

2. The movie really <u>had an impact on</u> her. She couldn't stop crying after she watched it.

    a. had an effect on   b. had a purpose for

3. The correct answer was so <u>obvious</u> that everyone in the class got it right.

    a. difficult to find   b. easy to understand

4. This unusual <u>device</u> is a machine used for cutting designs in wood products.

    a. material   b. piece of equipment

5. The Hope Diamond is <u>unique</u> because there is no other large diamond in the world that is such a dark blue color.

    a. commonly found   b. only one of its kind

6. Practicing every day is an <u>integral</u> part of learning to play the piano.

    a. necessary   b. unusual

(continued)

7. Sam didn't have the right tools to do the job <u>adequately</u> so the table he built fell apart.

    a. on time   b. well enough

8. <u>Concentration</u> is required when you are taking notes, so please pay careful attention to what the speaker is saying.

    a. focus   b. encouragement

9. Sarah is a computer <u>technician</u>. She is very skilled at creating new software programs.

    a. professor   b. specialist

10. We need to find an <u>innovative</u> way to advertise this product—an idea that no one has ever used before.

    a. original   b. typical

11. It takes a lot of <u>coordination</u> to dance, sing, and act all at once.

    a. the ability to move smoothly   b. great physical strength

12. Pilots can use an automatic computer system to fly a plane, but they also have the option of turning it off and flying the plane <u>manually</u>.

    a. according to instructions in a book   b. physically; by oneself

13. In order to <u>master</u> the skill of cooking and become an expert, you have to spend a lot of time in the kitchen.

    a. invent a new way of doing something   b. become highly skilled at doing something

14. Some robots are designed to be life-like. They are built to <u>simulate</u> the movements of humans.

    a. copy; reproduce   b. make active; speed up

While You Listen

First Listening

A. 🎧 *Listen to the first half of the lecture about Foley artists. Complete the notes. Then check your answers with your teacher. Remember to omit any unimportant or unnecessary words.*

> **Useful Terms**
>
> **synchronize:** to do something exactly at the same time.
>
> **Example**
> ·········
>
> > **Please record and synchronize** *the sound of a door closing so that it happens when the actor on the screen is closing the door.*

Foley Artists: Who's Making that Noise?

Introduction:

Sound effects (SFX): integral part - movie watching experience

       - reinforce emotional impact & tell story

I. SFX - usually produced by (1) _____ & sound-processing software

some SFX - most advanced equipment (2) _____ adequately

record, reproduce (example - soft movement of (3) _____ &

(4) _____ in snow)

A. expert needed - sound technician = Foley artist

    1. term Foley from earliest & famous Hollywood (5) _____

    expert - Jack Foley

      a. produced innovative & synchronized SFX - sounds exactly

      (6) _____

II. Foley SFX - created manually by Foley artist at (7) _____

(projected)

A. Created to go with (8) _____ caused by (9) _____ in real time

    1. realistic match (10) _____ sound with action on screen

      a. (11) _____ & carefully follow (12) _____ of

      actors (example - actor opens door, Foley artist make sound of opening

      exact same time)

      b. requires lots concentration & physical coordination

      c. master art of Foley - study (13) _____ &

      (14) _____

III. Foley artist job - create (15) _____, (16) _____ SFX

(example - sound of eggs breaking, drinking water quickly)

    A. (17) _____ use (18) _____ eggs or record

    someone drinking water

    B. collect large variety of (19) _____ - simulate sound of

    action, object

    C. Successful - look at object & (20) _____

B. 🎧 **On Your Own** *Listen to the second half of the lecture. Complete the notes. Remember to omit any unimportant or unnecessary information.*

IV. Foley recording studio - looks like place threw out garbage

   A. _____

   B. _____

   (example -   )

   C. _____

V. Existing or found objects not effective for right noise - Foley artist build own devices

   (example - create sound wind: cloth stretched over drum made of small, separate wood boards - drum goes around, spins against cloth - realistic sound of wind)

   A. _____

   B. Professional - dozen or more boxes with doors

      1. _____ -

VI. Stage in floor of Foley artist's studio

   A. Stage - _____ -

   (example - stone, wood, metal)

      1. _____

   B. Many different kinds of shoes needed

      1. _____

VII. Realistic quality of Foley SFX -

   A. _____

C. *Compare your notes from the second half of the lecture with a partner. Then discuss these questions together.*

   1. How are your notes different? How are they similar?

   2. Did you include any unnecessary words or information? What were they?

Second Listening

🎧 **Check Your Notes** *Listen and check your notes from the First Listening. Add any information you missed or change any incorrect information. Then check your answers with your teacher.*

After You Listen

■ EXERCISE 1

A. *Use your notes from the Second Listening to answer the questions in the chart. Omit any unnecessary words, but do try to list as many details and examples as you can.*

I. How did Foley artists get their name? Who was this person?	II. How do Foley artists synchronize sound?	III. What do they use to make SFX?
	watch & carefully follow actors' movements	garbage - useless things:

B. *Work with a partner. Compare your answers for Exercise A. Then check your answers with your teacher.*

■ EXERCISE 2

Work in pairs. Discuss these questions.

1. Do you think sound effects are important in movies and television shows? Why?

2. Do you notice sound effects when you watch movies or television? If you don't, why do you think you don't pay attention to them?

3. Do you think being a Foley artist would be a fun job? Explain.

■ EXERCISE 3

Work in groups. Create a role play with your own sound effects. Then perform it for the class. Follow these instructions:

1. Write a short story that has a lot of action and different characters for each person in your group. Think about what sound effects you would like to use to illustrate the actions.

2. Decide what sound effects you need for your role play. Collect classroom objects and your own belongings to create the sound effects or search the Internet for computer sound effects you can download and use (use search words such as *free sound effects*).

3. Perform your role play for your class and have one or two classmates make the sound effects you have chosen at the proper time.

UNIT 3
Using Abbreviations and Symbols

Unit Warm Up

If you use email or send and receive text messages, you probably already use symbols and abbreviations. Look at the quiz below and try to guess what these common abbreviations and symbols mean and then check your answers with your teacher.

Email and Text Messaging Quiz

_____ 1. : - D   a. got to go

_____ 2. CM   b. surprised

_____ 3. B4N   c. talk to you later

_____ 4. :- o   d. sounds like a plan

_____ 5. LMK   e. laugh out loud

_____ 6. T+   f. smiling

_____ 7. W?   g. let me know

_____ 8. SLAP   h. bye for now

_____ 9. LOL   i. call me

_____ 10. G2G   j. why

SKILL PRESENTATION

Taking notes is a little like text messaging on a cell phone. When you are listening to a lecture, you do not have enough time to write down every word you hear, so it's a good idea to learn how to replace words with symbols and to use abbreviations to make words shorter. By practicing this important skill, you can take good notes much faster.

Abbreviations

Abbreviations are one way to shorten words. There are several ways to abbreviate words.

1. Use only the first syllable.

   Examples

   pol = politics   *del = delete*   *chem = chemical*

2. Use the first syllable and one or two letters of the next syllable.

   Examples

   bio = biology   *subj = subject*   *repr = represent*

3. Omit the final letters.

   Examples

   assoc = associate   *univ = university*   *indiv = individual*

4. Omit vowels but keep enough consonants so you still recognize the word.

   Examples

   prblm = problem   *gvt = government*   *bckgrd = background*

5. Write out in full the name of the person, place, or title of an organization or business the first time you hear it. When it is repeated, use the initials.

   Examples

   William Shakespeare = WS   *New York City = NYC*

   National Aeronautics and Space Administration = NASA

Symbols

Symbols are a very quick way to note important information. You probably already know many common mathematical symbols; however, it is worth the time to learn as many other types of symbols as you can.

Some standard abbreviations and symbols are as follows:

Symbol	Meaning	Abbreviation	Meaning
+ or &	and; plus; in addition; also; more	w/	with
@	at	w/o	without
→	leads to; produces; causes; makes	b/4	before
←	comes from; is the result of	b/c	because
↑	increases; goes up; rises	i.e.	in other words
↓	decreases; goes down; lowers	e.g. or ex	for example/example/such as
/	per	etc.	and so on; and other things
=	is; means; equal to; same as	re	regarding; about; concerning
≠	is not; doesn't mean; different	esp	especially
#	number	min.	minimium; the least possible amount, degree, or number
>	is greater than		
<	is less than	max.	maximum; the greatest possible amount, degree, or number
∴	therefore; so		
%	percent	p/pp	page/pages
"	inches	ft	feet
'	minute (also min)	kg	kilogram
°	degree	lb	pound
~ or ±	about; approximately; more or less	m	meter
" "	ditto; repeated words	yr	year
♀	woman; female	pro	for; agree with; in favor of
♂	man; male	con	against; disagree with; opposed to

■ **EXERCISE 1**

A. *Study just the abbreviations in the chart above. Then work with a partner. Cover the explanations in the right-hand column of Exercise 1 on the next page. Tell your partner what the abbreviations mean. Then change roles.*

B. *Study just the symbols in the chart above. Then work with a partner. Cover the explanations in the right-hand column of Exercise 2 on the next page. Tell your partner what the symbols mean. Then change roles.*

PRACTICE

Match the abbreviations in the left-hand column with their meanings in the column on the right.

_i_	1. esp	a.	different
___	2. lrg	b.	usually
___	3. SF	c.	hours
___	4. ed	d.	black
___	5. diff	e.	flexible
___	6. fr	f.	education
___	7. grp	g.	last
___	8. hrs	h.	large
___	9. usu	i.	especially
___	10. flex	j.	group
___	11. lst	k.	from
___	12. blk	l.	San Francisco

■ EXERCISE 2

Match the symbols in the left-hand column with their meanings in the column on the right.

_c_	1. /	a.	and; plus; in addition; also; more
___	2. #	b.	increases; goes up; rises
___	3. ♂	c.	per
___	4. <	d.	dollars
___	5. +	e.	woman; female
___	6. @	f.	is; means; equal to; same as
___	7. ↑	g.	number
___	8. $	h.	ditto; repeated words
___	9. " "	i.	degree
___	10. ♀	j.	is less than
___	11. =	k.	at
___	12. °	l.	man; male

🎧 *Listen to a lecture about the ocean and its animals. Complete the notes below with abbreviations or symbols from the box.*

b/c	lb	pro	&	∴
con	kg	re	→	%
ex	m	w/o	←	~
ft	max	yr	≠	" "
>	↓	↑		#

1. Prof. Smith talk _re_ ocean & its animals

2. scientists claim ~ 80 % ocean pollut ____ land

3. cool weather & heavy rainfl → fish pop ____

4. marine creatures **w/o** eyesight, ____ blind goby fsh can hunt food

5. grouper fsh live **max** 80 - 100 ____

6. squid ____ octopus squid = 10 arms & octop. = 8 " "

7. giant nomura's jellyfsh grow up to 65 ____ or 2 **m** long

8. jellyfsh weigh **max** 450 **lbs** or 220 ____

9. people hurt by jellyfsh ____ by sharks

10. lmt commerc. ocean fshg: **pro** fsh pop. = nearly disappear ____ over-fshg

11. lmt commerc.fshg: **con** people lose jobs ____ economy hurt if can't fsh

12. imprt ____ awarenss of lrg **#** people **re** dangr of destroy ocean environ

Note
Use standard symbols and abbreviations but also feel free to make up your own. However, be sure you can understand the ones you make up later when you review your notes.

A. 🎧 *Listen. You will hear an introduction to a lecture about jellyfish. Take notes. Use the symbols and abbreviations you have practiced in this unit (and create some of your own).*

_____

_____

_____

_____

_____

_____

_____

_____

_____

_____

_____

B. *Compare your notes with a partner. Then check your answers with your teacher.*

LISTENING TASK

Before You Listen

Portuguese Man-of-War

sail
(ruffled ridge at top)

gas-filled float
(bubble-like body)

tentacles
(arm-like structures hanging from float)

Sea Wasp

bell
(box-shaped body)

tentacles
(arm-like structures hanging from bell)

A. Topic Preview *Work in pairs. Use the pictures of the jellyfish on page 126 to discuss these questions. Then share your ideas with the class.*

1. The jellyfish on the left is called a *Portuguese Man-of-War* because it looks a little like a type of warship with the same name. Why do you think the jellyfish on the right is called a *Sea Wasp*? (Hint: a "wasp" is similar to a bee.)

2. What do you think these jellyfish use their tentacles (arms) for?

3. How are the two jellyfish different from each other? How are they similar?

4. Have you ever seen a jellyfish at the ocean or in an aquarium? If so, discuss the experience and describe the jellyfish you saw.

B. Vocabulary Preview *Match the words to their definitions. Use a dictionary if necessary. Then use the words to complete the sentences on the next page.*

_____*j*_____ 1. bubble

_____ 2. poison

_____ 3. trigger

_____ 4. complex

_____ 5. float

_____ 6. transparent

_____ 7. deadly

_____ 8. gracefully

_____ 9. reaction

_____ 10. consequence

_____ 11. invisible

_____ 12. prey

_____ 13. enormous

_____ 14. flexible

a. an animal or animals that are hunted, killed, and eaten by another animal

b. a result; outcome

c. having the ability to kill; fatal

d. a response to something or someone; an effect

e. able to bend, curve, or twist

f. any substance that harms or kills when you eat, drink, or touch it

g. not able to be seen

h. clear; see-through

i. very large; huge

j. a small, transparent ball of gas or air, usually on top of or in a liquid such as water

k. having the ability to move smoothly and easily

l. having many parts or details, usually working together or related

m. to stay on top of water or other liquids without going under

n. to start, cause, produce, activate

(continued)

15. The glass container is _____ so you can see the candy inside of it.

16. As a _____ of not wearing a hat in the sun, people get sunburns on their heads.

17. Mice are common _____ for cats on a farm.

18. Ballroom dancers move _____ with beautiful steps and style.

19. This household cleaner is a _____. It will harm children if they accidentally drink it.

20. If you can put your foot behind your head, then you are very _____.

21. Some tiny insects are so light that they can _____ on top of the water.

22. An _____ pizza, measuring 122 feet, 8 inches in diameter, was baked in 1990 in South Africa.

23. A bite from a Black Mamba snake can be _____, causing the victim to die in about 20 minutes.

24. A typical _____ to drinking coffee or tea is to feel more awake.

25. Sunshine in the morning will _____ some flowers to open.

26. An automobile is more _____ than a bicycle because it has so many more parts.

27. You can't see music when you hear it, so it is _____.

28. The dishwashing soap made a large _____ when I added the water to it.

While You Listen

Remember

Be sure your notes include the **key words**—the words that have the most important meaning. These are the main ideas and other important details such as numbers, times, and dates. For example, imagine you hear the speaker say:

"One effect caused by global warming is that worldwide sea levels are rising by 1.7 to 1.8 millimeters per year."

The following key words and details might be included in your notes:

Globl warmg → ww sea lev ↑1.7–1.8 mm/yr

First Listening

A. 🎧 **Guided Practice** *Listen to the first half of the lecture. Complete the left column of the chart below. (You will complete the right column later.) Then check your answers with your teacher.*

> *Useful Terms*
>
> **sting:** to make a hole in the skin of an animal or person and release a chemical that causes a painful, burning feeling
>
> > *Example*
> >
> > *Bees and other insects* **sting** *when they feel they are in danger.*
>
> **jellyfish stingers:** small, sharp, hooked organs located inside jellyfish tentacles, which, when touched or triggered by a chemical, shoot poison into fish or people who come into contact with them
>
> > *Example*
> >
> > *The swimmer felt a sharp pain in his leg. It was caused by the poison from the jellyfish stingers.*

Poisonous Jellyfish: Who's Afraid to Go into the Water?

Intro - Jellyfish: -enorm. vari of fantstic

shape (1) _____ size

- found oceans (2) _____
  fr. Australia — Alaska

- 2 poison jf = Portuguese
  Man-of-War (MOW) & Sea
  Wasp (SW) (3) _____

MOW: -lives:

(4) _____ & Atlan oceans,
Mediterr & Caribb Sea & Gulf of
Mexi

- tiny sail: allws (5) _____
  to move

- color: (6) _____ blu or
  prple

SW: > deadly MOW

    < commn MOW =

- found in _____

_____

_____

- tentcl: _____

_____

- stingr: _____

_____

_____

- size: _____

_____

_____

(continued)

- tentacle: use to catch prey
  (7) _____ fish/other sea
  creature, flex & stretch
  (8) _____ ocean = 165
  (9) _____ contact →
  terrible

  - stingr: series of 1000s run ↓
    length of each tentcl

touch by prey/human arm/leg =
trigger to shoot (10) _____ &
hked stingrs full of poison

sing tentcl = (11) _____ = 10s
of mil/jf

swimmrs describe sting = bee attack
or shock by electricty = pain contin
(12) _____

- poison: full strength after froze
(13) _____

serious & deadly consequence = lrg.
red, raised (14) _____ on skin,
(15) _____ to go away

& (16) _____ breath probs heart
stop (reactions → kill swimmers far fr
shore)

no pic up on beach (17) _____
remembr: (18) _____ of 1 tencl
broke off = serious hurt

- good swimmer _____
  _____
  _____
- eyes: _____
  _____
  _____
- invis: _____
  _____
  _____
- sting: _____
  _____
  _____

Conclusion: _____
_____
_____
_____
_____

B. 🎧 **On Your Own** *Listen to the second half of the lecture. Complete the notes on pages 129–130 in the columns on the right.*

C. *Work with a partner. Compare your notes from Exercises A and B. Discuss these questions.*

1. Can you understand your notes?

2. How are your notes different? How are they similar?

3. Did you include all the key words?

D. *Check your notes with your teacher.*

Second Listening

🎧 **Check Your Notes** *Listen and check your notes from the First Listening. Add any information you missed or change any incorrect information. Then check your answers with your teacher.*

After You Listen

■ **EXERCISE 1**

A. *Indicate whether each statement is true about the Portuguese Man-of-War or the Sea Wasp. Check (✓) the correct boxes. Use your lecture notes to help you.*

	Man-of-War	Sea Wasp	
1.			is light blue or purple
2.			has poison that's full strength after being frozen for six years
3.			uses sail to float in wind
4.			is square-shaped
5.			has groups of eyes
6.			releases stingers when touched
7.			has tentacles with 5,000 stingers each
8.			has poison that can kill 60 adults in three minutes
9.			can swim fast
10.			has 60 tentacles
11.			is transparent
12.			has tentacles that stretch up to 165 feet
13.			lives in the Gulf of Mexico
14.			floats on top of the water

B. *Work with a partner. Check your answers with your teacher. Then make a list of any original symbols or abbreviations that you created for your notes. Why did you use those symbols or abbreviations? Were they helpful in answering the questions above?*

C. *Work in groups. Discuss these questions.*

1. What else would you like to know about poisonous jellyfish?

2. What are some other kinds of poisonous animals or insects? How do they protect themselves with their poison?

3. Have you ever been stung by a poisonous animal or an insect? What happened? What did you do?

4. Do you know of any home treatments for dealing with bites or stings? Have you tried them?

UNIT 4

Determining What's Important

Unit Warm Up

Read the following sentence taken from a lecture. Why is the underlined part of the sentence important? What does the information after the underlined phrase tell you about the lecture?

The speaker says: "Let me start off today with a discussion of investigation techniques."

SKILL PRESENTATION 1

Learning to listen for important information is a lot like learning to read effectively. When you read for specific information, your eyes look for words and expressions that will help you understand the important ideas. When you listen, you can train your ears to do the same thing—to listen for specific "signal" words and expressions. Signal words and expressions are like traffic signals that tell you to stop, go, or change direction. They give you a road map for what you should or should not write down in your notes.

> **Note**
> Speakers often use a blackboard, whiteboard, a flip chart, or a computer slide projection to list especially important information. Pay careful attention to this information and be sure to write the key words and phrases in your notes.

Topic Signals

Usually lectures and talks are well organized with an introduction, a body with supporting ideas and details, and a conclusion. Sometimes a speaker will begin by reviewing previous information. Let's look at some general expressions that will give you clues to how lecture topics are organized. Understanding the organization will help you organize the most important information in your notes in a logical way.

Review of a Previous Topic

A speaker sometimes uses expressions to remind listeners what was discussed previously and to review any important information. This is a good reason to review your own notes from the previous lecture, as it will help you relate the prior information to the current lecture.

Examples

If you **recall** from **last week** …

You **remember** that we discussed X …

In the **last lecture**, you heard about X …

Last time, we were talking about X …

Introduction of the Main Topic

A speaker may use expressions to tell the listeners about the main idea of the lecture. Listening for these expressions will help you focus on the important topics the speaker will discuss so you can better organize your notes. These introductory expressions are generally used near the beginning of a lecture, so be ready to start writing your notes as soon as the speaker begins.

Examples

Today, *we will be discussing / talking about* …

Let me **start off** today *with* …

What I will be **focusing on** / **dealing with** *in this lecture is* …

I'd like to discuss **two things today.** *The* **first** *is* … *and the* **second** *is* …

Change of Topic

A speaker may also use expressions to introduce a new topic or a supporting idea. Hearing these expressions signals that you need to indicate a new point in your notes by indenting, numbering, or lettering it (see Part 3, Unit 1, pages 101–103).

Examples

So now *we're going to discuss a* **new** *concept / idea* …

Now, *let's take a look at the* **next** *important point / issue / step* …

Let's **turn our attention** *to* …

This **brings us to** *the topic of* …

Let's **move on** *to* …

Conclusion/Summary of Topic

Some expressions tell the listeners that the speaker is finishing the lecture and may repeat or review the main points. This is a great opportunity to write down in your notes any of the main points you might have missed before. These final notes can also be used for a quick review later.

Examples

So, *to* **summarize** / **conclude** / **wrap up** / **sum up** …

OK, *let's* **review** *what we've discussed today* …

Finally, *we can* **conclude** *our discussion today by* …

PRACTICE

■ EXERCISE 1

Follow these instructions:

1. Read the lecture on crime scene investigation. Pay attention to the main ideas.

2. Read the lecture again quickly and circle the topic signals.

3. Write the type of topic signal above each one: Write review (review the previous topic), intro (introduce the main topic), change (change the topic), or concl (conclusion).

Good morning everyone. OK, so, for those of you who attended the really

review

interesting guest lecture, (if you recall from last week,) the speaker had discussed the best

ways to report a crime. Oh, and let me digress for a moment here—the speaker, Officer

Thompson, mentioned how much he appreciated the thoughtful questions some of you

asked … maybe we can invite him back again? OK, to get back to the subject at hand.

What I'll be focusing on in this lecture is a detailed examination of how the process of

crime scene investigation works.

Let me start off today with an explanation of what crime scene investigation is. So,

exactly what is crime scene investigation? Well, crime scene investigation, or as it is

commonly referred to, CSI, is defined as a long and detailed process that involves a careful

and focused recording of the conditions at the scene of a crime. This process also consists

of collecting any physical objects, marks, or other signs that could possibly explain what

happened and point to who did it. To put it another way, crime scene investigation brings

together science, logic, and law.

That brings us to the topic of the specific kind of objects, marks, or other signs that the

CSI team collects and studies. So, what do we mean by these three things exactly? Well, for

example, everything from a human hair and clothing to furniture that has been knocked

over or is not in the right place. Certain kinds of marks or impressions that can be used as

(continued)

physical proof. For instance, foot- or fingerprints or marks left by tools on a door or those left by car tires in the dirt. Electronic devices, such as a telephone answering machine, are also considered significant. What I'm trying to say is that anything, inside or outside a crime scene, is important for helping to catch a criminal.

Now, let's take a look at the first step in the process: a CSI investigator arrives at the scene—in this case, an apartment where someone has broken in and stolen things. First, the investigator makes sure that it is safe and stops other people from entering. She then walks through the apartment to get a general feeling about the crime scene. And, by the way, the investigator talks to the people on the scene to find out if anyone has moved anything. So, OK, let's return to what we were talking about. Perhaps next, the investigator comes up with a general theory based on what she can see and notes any physical objects, marks, or signs that might be useful. However, she does not touch anything yet.

Now, let's turn our attention to another step in the process: documentation. This means that the investigator makes a record of the scene by taking photographs or drawing pictures. Again, she still does not touch a thing. Oh, and I forgot to mention that sometimes the entire crime scene is recorded on video.

OK, so to wrap up the process, the investigator, step-by-step, carefully collects all the possible physical proof, like broken glass or pieces of clothing torn and left on the window, and so on. She labels each piece—that is, she writes the date, location, and other information on a label attached to it—then she writes all the labels down on a list and puts each piece in a separate package to be sent to a laboratory for further scientific investigation.

SKILL PRESENTATION 2

Other Types of Topic Signals

Digressions and Return to Topic

Most lectures or talks are organized in a logical pattern; however, sometimes a speaker will skip to another topic. This means he or she is digressing, or going away from the main point. When you take notes, you should try to recognize when digressions are important and when they are not. Listen for expressions similar to the following to help you decide what to include in your notes and what to leave out.

Possible Important Digressions

Some digressions are important because they add information that the speaker forgot to mention or they are in response to comments or questions from the listeners.

Examples

> *Now,* before *I* go on …
>
> By the way …
>
> *OK, let me talk about X* for a minute …
>
> *Oh, and I* forgot to mention *that* …
>
> *That* reminds *me* …
>
> *Let me just* go back *and explain that a little further* …

Possible Unimportant Digressions

Other digressions can be personal stories, jokes, or even opinions and so, they are not necessarily important for you to write in your notes.

Examples

> *Let me* digress *for a moment* …
>
> *Oh, that* reminds *me* of *a funny story / joke I heard* …
>
> *This is* an aside, *but I remember the time that I* …
>
> Did you see *the movie / television show about X?*
>
> *You can decide for yourself, but* in my opinion …

Return to Topic

Thankfully, the speaker will usually signal a return to the main topic by using expressions such as these, so you will know when your notes should go back to main topic.

Examples

Anyway, back to / let's return to *what we were talking about* ...

What *were we* talking about*? Oh, yeah, I was saying* ...

Where were we*?

OK, to get back *to the* subject at hand ...

PRACTICE

■ EXERCISE 2

Follow these instructions:

1. Look again at the crime scene investigation lecture on pages 135–136. This time, circle the topic signals for "unimportant digressions," "important digressions," and "return to topic."
2. In the space above each topic signal, label each signal "unimprt digress," "imprt digress" or "return."
3. Underline the information following each signal that you should write down in your notes. Remember: Do not underline information that is not important.

SKILL PRESENTATION 3

Extended Definition Signals

Now that we've looked at some more general topic signals, let's move on to a more specific pattern of organization. (By the way, that sentence just told you there is going to be a topic change, and this sentence is a digression.)

When speakers need to explain a difficult concept or a complicated process, they frequently organize their lectures using an extended definition pattern. With this type of organization, the main topic is quickly defined at the beginning and then the lecture continues with a more detailed description, including examples. A speaker might use several different signal words and expressions when defining the main topic.

Definition of Main Topic

Listen carefully for the following types of signals at the beginning of a lecture to understand what the main topic is and how it is defined. Some common phrases that are often used to define the main topic are *defined as, consists of, composed of, made up of, seems to be, means, is/are.*

Taking notes on the examples you hear will help you understand any difficult concepts or processes when you study your notes later. Listen for the following types of signals:

Examples

For example, ...　　　　　　　　　*such as, ...*

For instance, ...　　　　　　　　　*Imagine ...*

To illustrate / As an illustration, ...　　*In this case, ...*

like...

Clarifications

Speakers want their listeners to understand what they are saying. They use the following types of signals to make a point clearer or clarify it by repeating the same idea in more simple terms or with additional information:

Examples

What I'm trying to say is ...　　　　*That is, ...*

What I mean is ...　　　　　　　　*To put it another way, ...*

Rhetorical Questions

Rhetorical questions are used to signal an introduction to a topic, focus attention on important details, or give an example or definition of something. They are not questions in the standard sense because listeners are not expected to offer answers. Speakers usually follow this type of question with their own answers.

Listen for rising intonation at the end of a sentence to hear these questions and then carefully note the information the speaker gives to answer the rhetorical question. Notice that many of these questions begin with a *wh-* word:

Examples

Do/Did you know ....?　　　　　*So, exactly what is ...?*

Why do you think X is ...?　　　　*How can we define X?*

What do we mean by X?　　　　*Where can X be found/seen?*

PRACTICE

■ EXERCISE 3

A. 🎧 **Listen to some sentences from the lecture on crime scene investigation. Write the topic signals you hear for definitions of topics, examples, clarifications, and rhetorical questions.**

1. _So, exactly what is...?_
2. _____
3. _____
4. _____
5. _____
6. _____
7. _____
8. _____
9. _____
10. _____
11. _____
12. _____

B. **Work with a partner. After each topic signal in Exercise A, write the type. Use these abbreviations: def (definition), ex (example), clarif (clarification), or rhetor (rhetorical).**

LISTENING TASK

Before You Listen

A. Topic Preview *Work in groups. Look at the following pictures and discuss these questions.*

1. How do you think fingerprints like those in the pictures are made?

2. Who do you think uses fingerprints? Why?

3. Why do you think fingerprints might be more useful for finding out who someone is than a photograph of that person?

4. Have you ever seen fingerprints being taken or being used? Where? What was the reason they were being taken or used?

Three Basic Fingerprint Patterns

LOOP   ARCH   WHORL

B. Vocabulary Preview *Read the sentences. Then write each underlined word next to its definition on the next page.*

• This is the first time I've tried this dance step, so it's really <u>challenging</u> for me.

• John needs a new watch. His isn't <u>accurate</u>, so he misses the bus every day.

• Look! The top of the mountain is finally <u>visible</u> above the clouds.

• The elephant left a clear <u>impression</u> of its foot in the wet sand by the river.

• Please look at this photograph and <u>identify</u> the person you saw running away.

• A <u>reliable</u> friend is one who will always be there if you need help.

• That sign keeps falling down. Please find a better way to <u>secure</u> it to the wall.

• Our <u>procedure</u> for reporting vacation days isn't working. We need to find another way.

• Tigers have a <u>distinctive</u> pattern of stripes that make them different from other cats.

• Can you <u>obtain</u> all the documents you need to get your passport by the end of the month?

(continued)

- In her cookbook, the chef decided to <u>reveal</u> that coffee is the secret ingredient.
- The crime investigator collected the human hair on the coat as <u>evidence</u> for the police.
- People in the United States use different words to say hello. One <u>variation</u> used in the state of Texas is "howdy."
- These instructions have 25 steps to follow. They are just too <u>complicated</u> for me.

1. _____*distinctive*_____ different for each individual thing; only one of its kind
2. _____ to know or recognize someone and say who that person is
3. _____ can be trusted or depended on
4. _____ get; to find
5. _____ having many different parts; difficult to understand or deal with
6. _____ a specific or correct method of doing something
7. _____ can be seen; noticeable
8. _____ not easy; difficult
9. _____ physical proof; objects, marks, or signs used to prove facts
10. _____ a change or difference from what is usual or common
11. _____ exact; correct; true
12. _____ a mark or pattern made when something hard is pushed into something softer
13. _____ to show; to make known
14. _____ to firmly attach, connect, or fix to something

While You Listen

First Listening

A. 🎧 **Guided Practice** *Listen to the first half of the talk. Complete the notes. Then check your answers with a partner.*

> **Useful Term**
> **criminal suspect:** a person who is believed to have committed a crime, such as stealing something, but who has not actually been proven to have done the crime
>
> **Example**
>
> *The police said that there are several* **criminal suspects** *whose fingerprints were found at the crime scene.*

The Science of Fingerprinting

Introduction:

Previous topic: Main topic(s):

(1) _____   (2) _____

_____

Definition & Patterns:

   Definition of topic: (1) _____

   curving lines: (2) _____

_____

      Loop pattern: (3) _____

_____

           (4) _____ pattern: (5) _____

            (ex. - (6) _____

_____)

     Arch pattern: (7) _____

_____

         (ex - (8) _____

_____)

 3 basic patterns → (9) _____

_____

       (ex- _____

_____)

Why used:

   Usefl & accurate b/c each indiv (1) _____

_____

     (clarification) (2) _____

_____

fingrprnt not (3) _____

     (clarification) (4) _____

_____

B. 🎧 *Listen to the second half of the talk. Complete the notes. Then check your answers with a partner.*

Procedure to obtain:

CSI investigtr search for (1) _____ fingrprnt:
some can see and others are (2) _____

Visible: found on (3) _____
left when (4) _____
_____

  - Molded fingrprnt: (5) _____
  _____

  - Latent fingrprnt: ++challenge left by (6) _____
  _____

b/c (7) _____ investigtr use exper to locate (8) _____
_____

(ex - (9) _____
_____
_____)

Techniq for collect:

Most common: (1) _____ use to mark
fingrprnt on (2) _____ surfaces
powdr = (3) _____
_____ apply (4) _____
after brush powdr on prnt (5) _____
tape + prnt (6) _____
_____

  (techniq) called (7) dusting _____
  (8) _____ process & 1 involve heat up super glue also used to
  (9) _____

Conclusion:

Summary = (1) _____

_____ so _____

Crime scene investigatr look for (2) _____ & _____

fingrprnt use (3) _____

Next lecture topic = (4) _____

_____

C. **Work with a partner. Compare your notes from the First Listening. Then discuss these questions.**

1. Did you listen for signal words? Were they useful for helping you hear what information to write down in your notes?

2. Were you able to understand and write down all the examples? Do you remember any phrases the speaker used to signal examples? If so, what were they?

3. Did you notice any information in the talk that you did **not** need to write down? Explain.

Second Listening

Check Your Notes *Listen and check your notes from the First Listening. Add any information you missed or change any incorrect information. Then check your answers with your teacher.*

Tip
Listen for other words and phrases that indicate the important ideas of the lecture.

Examples

Numbered lists: First, second, third, *or* five important points

Repetition: To repeat, let me repeat that, *or* once again, let's review

Adding ideas: another, also, in addition, too

Opposing ideas: however, on the other hand, but

After You Listen

Writing a summary means using your own words to express only the main ideas and the most important details of what you heard. Creating a summary is an excellent way to remember and confirm that you understood the lecture. You can also use it to review for a test. Try to write a summary as soon as possible after hearing a lecture.

■ **EXERCISE 1**

Use your notes from the First Listening to complete the summary. Use as few words as possible.

Crime scene investigators collect _____ *fingerprints for evidence* _____. Fingerprints
                                                                        (1)

are _____ of the skin and of the fingers. There are _____
           (2)   **(3)**

basic patterns consisting of _____ and _____: the loop,
                                          (4)   **(5)**

_____, and _____. Based on these three patterns, the skin
         (6)   **(7)**

can create billions of unique patterns. Fingerprints are a very good way to identify people

because _____. Also, fingerprints don't change _____.
                 (8)   **(9)**

CSI investigators search for _____ kinds of fingerprints; some
                                          (10)

_____ and some _____. _____ can be seen
         (11)   **(12)**   **(13)**

on smooth surfaces. _____ are marks left in soft
                                    (14)

things, and _____, which are usually _____ to see, are left
                    (15)   **(16)**

by marks made by skin oil or other body fluids. There are also _____
                                                                                   (17)

techniques for collecting fingerprints. The first one, _____, uses a
                                                                    (18)

brush to put _____ powder on a print in circles until you can see
                    (19)

it. Then, _____ to pick the print up, it is _____
                 (20)   **(21)**

and then put on _____ for the police. A _____
                        (22)   **(23)**

and one that involves _____ are also used to
                                    (24)

_____.
         (25)

Now it's your turn to be an investigator. Complete the following project in a small group.

A. *Collect your own fingerprints. Follow these instructions.*

You will need:

1. transparent drinking glasses or smooth bottles
2. cooking oil or hand lotion
3. cocoa powder
4. transparent, sticky tape
5. a few small, soft brushes
6. sheets of light-colored construction paper

Procedure:

1. Put a tiny amount of oil or hand lotion on the pad* of one finger (usually the first finger or the thumb make a good print). Rub most of it off.

2. Lightly press your oily finger pad on the side of a drinking glass or bottle. This works best if you can roll the finger from one side to the other.

2. Dust or sprinkle from above (don't touch the glass) some cocoa powder on the oily fingerprint. Make sure it is well covered.

3. Brush (in a circular motion) the cocoa-covered fingerprint very softly with a brush until you see it appear.

4. Place the sticky side of the tape on the dusted fingerprint and carefully lift the tape.

5. Press the tape with the fingerprint onto a piece of construction paper.

6. Ask each person in the group to write his or her name on the paper next to the fingerprint.

7. Repeat if you don't get a clear print. Try cleaning your hands and fingers (do not use oil or lotion) if the print doesn't come out right.

* The pad is on the underside of the finger. It is the round area between the top of the finger and the first joint or the first line where the finger bends.

B. *Compare your fingerprints with your group members. Discuss these questions.*

1. What kinds of patterns do you see? For example, in which direction do the loops curve—toward the right or the left? Compare the size of the patterns (for example, how many ridges make up a loop).

2. Using the pictures of the three basic patterns on page 141, try to determine which type of fingerprint each of your group members has (loop, whorl, or arch).

3. Are your patterns different in any way from the three basic patterns? If so, explain how they are different.

C. *With your group, make a chart or table that lists the number of people with each type of print.*

D. *Ask all the groups in the class to combine the information from their charts and write it on the board. Then discuss the following questions.*

1. Which is the most common fingerprint pattern in your class?

2. Which is the least common pattern in your class?

3. Are there any unusual or unique patterns?

This unit will help you review the skills and strategies you learned in Part 3, Units 1 through 4, and will help you think about how you can continue to improve your note-taking.

Remember

When taking notes:
1. Choose a **format** that works the best for the main topic of the lecture:
   outline format—for talks organized by a series of events or steps or by a list of features or
   column format—for cause/effect, comparison/contrast, and problem/solution organization
2. Write the **main ideas** on the left (or in the left column) and the **details** on the right (or in the right column).
3. Focus on writing down **content words**—words that contain the most important information about the content of the lecture.
4. **Do not** use full sentences and **do not** try to write down every word you hear: Omit words that don't contain important meaning.
5. Use **abbreviations and symbols** in your notes. (See Part 3, Unit 3, pages 122–125.)
6. Listen for **signal words** and **expressions** that tell you what is important to include in your notes. (See Part 3, Unit 4, pages 133–138.)

Preparation is an integral part of taking good notes. Before you hear a lecture, read any materials about the topic that have been assigned or suggested.

A. *Read the text about swimmer Lynne Cox and underline the information that you think is most important.*

Lynne Cox is a very special, brave, and talented swimmer. She has faced the threat of large sharks, been stung by jellyfish, and swum in water cold enough to stop a normal person's heart. Here are just a few examples from her long list of extraordinary achievements:

Cox's first big swim was at the age of fourteen in 1971 near her home in southern California. She swam 26 miles (42 kilometers) from the coast south of Los Angeles to Catalina Island in 12 hours and 36 minutes. Returning to the same location again three years later, she broke both the men's and women's record: Her new time was 8 hours and 48 minutes—almost four hours less than her first swim.

By the age of seventeen, Cox had swum the English Channel (the narrow waterway that separates England from France) twice. Both times, she broke the women's and the men's world records. The second time, she set a new record by swimming the Channel in 9 hours and 36 minutes. Cox was also the first person to swim the waters of the Strait of Magellan near Chile, South America, and the first to swim around the Cape of Good Hope at the southern tip of Africa.

However, it was her 1987 swim in the Bering Strait, located in the far north between Alaska and Russia, that brought Cox international attention. She swam to promote peace between the United States and what was then the Soviet Union. It was the first time in 48 years that the border between the two countries had been opened up. The water temperature that Cox swam in (again, she was the first to do it) ranged from 38 degrees Fahrenheit to around 41 degrees Fahrenheit or 3 to 5 degrees Celsius. To put it another way, water this cold can be deadly, and she was in it for over 2 hours.

B. *Using the information you underlined in Exercise A, make brief notes on a separate piece of paper. Remember to use symbols and abbreviations. Check any new vocabulary words in a dictionary.*

> **Note**
> Degrees Fahrenheit and Celsius are usually abbreviated using the symbol for degree.
>
> **Examples**
>
> $32°F$ $15°C$

LISTENING TASK

Before You Listen

A. Vocabulary Preview *Work with a partner. Review these vocabulary words from Units 1 through 4. Take turns explaining them in your own words. Use a dictionary if necessary.*

adaptation (verb: *adapt*)	deadly	incredible	potentially	struggle
challenging (noun: *challenge*)	enormous	master	retain	unique
concentration (verb: *concentrate*)	float	metabolism	reveal	

B. Predict *You will hear a lecture about the swimmer Lynne Cox. Look at the speaker's notes on the board. What information do you think will be included in the lecture?*

open-water swimmer
Antarctica
Arctic near Alaska & Greenland
medical research—University of
   California at Santa Barbara
seal or penguin
core = center of body, including
   brain, heart, & lungs

While You Listen

In this section, you will hear a longer lecture divided into five parts. After each part, you will hear and answer some questions that will help you evaluate your note-taking skills.

Lynne Cox: An Amazing Long-Distance Swimmer

Evaluation Practice 1

A. 🎧 *Listen to the first part of the lecture about Lynne Cox and take notes on a separate piece of paper. Remember to review and use the information that the speaker has written on the board.*

> **Tip**
> The main topic of a lecture is usually stated at the beginning. Listen carefully for signal words and expressions that tell you about the main idea of the lecture.

B. 🎧 *Look at your notes from Exercise A. Listen and complete the evaluation. Use abbreviations and symbols in your answers.*

1. Main topic: unique ex how far push bdy to perfrm difficult cndition
2. Details: (1) _____
   (2) _____
3. a. column format   b. outline format
   Reason: _____

Evaluation Practice 2

A. 🎧 *Listen to the next part of the lecture and take notes on a separate piece of paper.*

> **Tip**
> If you chose the outline format, remember to write the main ideas on the left and then indent the details to the right. If you chose the column format, write the main ideas in the left column and the details in the right column.

B. 🎧 *Look at your notes from Exercise A. Listen and complete the evaluation.*
Use abbreviations and symbols in your answers.

1. Did you:

	Yes	No
label the columns (if you used the column format)?	☐	☐
number the main ideas and details?	☐	☐
indent details?	☐	☐
leave space after the main ideas and in the margins to add information or define terms later?	☐	☐

2. Answer:_____

3. Definition: _____

4. Answer (Cox's unusual body): _____

5. Check your notes (unnecessary words).

6. What is the new topic? _____

7. Abbreviations: _____

   _____

8. Check your notes (symbols).

Evaluation Practice 3

A. 🎧 *Listen to the next part of the lecture and take notes on a separate piece of paper.*

> **Tip**
> Don't worry if you miss a point. Consider asking the speaker, your classmates (or another person listening to the lecture) for the information later.

B. 🎧 *Look at your notes from Exercise A. Listen and complete the evaluation.*
Use abbreviations and symbols in your answers.

1. Main idea: _____

2. Did you:

	Yes	No
note the two unusual things researchers discovered about Cox's body?	☐	☐
note how these two things are balanced?	☐	☐
note how these two things help Cox swim better?	☐	☐

3. Symbols: _____

   _____

Evaluation Practice 4

A. 🎧 *Listen to the next part of the lecture and take notes on a separate piece of paper.*

> **Tip**
> Make sure you can understand the abbreviations and symbols that you used.

B. 🎧 *Look at your notes from Exercise A. Listen and complete the evaluation. Use abbreviations and symbols in your answers.*

1. Main idea: _____

2. Examples: _____

3. Did you:

	Yes	No
note the answer to the speaker's rhetorical question, "So, what does that mean exactly"?	☐	☐
omit personal pronouns (*he / she / they / it / them*)	☐	☐
omit demonstratives (*this / that / these / those*)	☐	☐
write down the most important content words	☐	☐

Evaluation Practice 5

A. 🎧 *Listen to the next part of the lecture and take notes on a separate piece of paper.*

B. 🎧 *Look at your notes from Exercise A. Listen and complete the evaluation. Use abbreviations and symbols in your answers.*

1. Purpose: _____

	Yes	No
2. Did you note the new information about how Cox controls the effects of cold water?	☐	☐

Self-Evaluation

A. *Think about your note-taking skills. In which areas do you feel confident? Which areas still need improvement? Check (✓) the columns to complete the self-evaluation.*

Unit 1 – Organizing Your Notes	Excellent	Good	Needs Improvement
Deciding which format to use (outline or column)			
Separating and organizing main ideas and details (indenting, labeling, columns, etc.)			
Leaving space for additional information			

Unit 2 – Omitting Unnecessary Words	Excellent	Good	Needs Improvement
Writing down only the most important content words			
Using your own words when possible			
Keeping descriptions and examples simple and brief			
Unit 3 – Using Abbreviations and Symbols	Excellent	Good	Needs Improvement
Using standard abbreviations and symbols			
Making up your own abbreviations and symbols and understanding them after the lecture			
Unit 4 – Determining What's Important	Excellent	Good	Needs Improvement
Listening for signal words and expressions for:			
- review of previous topic			
- topic introduced, changed, or concluded			
- definition of main topic			
- examples			
Digressions:			
- determining important or not important			
- hearing the speaker return to the topic afterward			
Listening for clarifications (signal for restated information)			
Understanding rhetorical questions (signal for important information)			

B. *For any skills that you feel you need to improve, go back and review the Skill Presentation sections in Part 2, Building Skills, before you go on to the next exercises.*

After You Listen

These exercises check how well you understand and can use the notes you took on the lecture about Lynne Cox.

■ EXERCISE 1

Not only is it important to prepare before you hear a talk or lecture, but it is also important to review.

Work with a partner. Using your notes, take turns explaining the lecture in your own words. As you listen to your partner, add any information you missed to your notes.

■ EXERCISE 2

If you took good, complete notes and can understand them well enough to answer questions, you will be able to answer questions about the lecture, for example, for a quiz or a test.

Using your notes, write T for true or F for false next to each statement. Then work with a partner to correct the false statements.

_F_ 1. The speaker says the topic she will be discussing today is Lynne Cox's career.

____ 2. Cox has adapted in ways that allow her to survive in difficult conditions.

____ 3. An open-water swimmer swims in lakes, rivers, and streams.

____ 4. Cox's record-setting, long-distance swims demonstrate how unique she is.

____ 5. The coldest water Cox swam in was the 28 degrees Fahrenheit water in the Arctic Ocean.

____ 6. Cox was fifty years old when she swam in the waters off Antarctica.

____ 7. Researchers discovered that Cox's body had 26 percent fat.

____ 8. Because of years of training, Cox developed very powerful muscles.

____ 9. A perfect balance of fat and muscle allows Cox to continue to swim forward.

____ 10. Cox has a layer of fat at the core (center) of her body.

____ 11. Cox survived by maintaining enough heat to keep her arms and legs warm.

____ 12. Cox's success is also due to the fact that she doesn't feel cold in the water.

Note-Taking Practice

In this unit, you will hear a long lecture and take notes completely on your own. This is your chance to use all the skills you have learned in Units 1 through 4. Based on the evaluations in Unit 5, focus on the skills that you feel need improvement as you take notes in this unit.

Unit Warm Up

If you can understand how a lecture or talk is organized, it will help you write clear, accurate notes that are easy to read and understand when you review them later. You studied various patterns of organization in Part 2 and have had practice taking notes on some of them in Part 3. In this unit, you will practice taking notes on a lecture that is organized by the cause/effect pattern.

Remember

In the cause/effect pattern, the main idea is that one event or action caused another to happen.

Example

I woke up late so I missed the bus.
cause   effect

Some of the signal words and phrases that indicate the speaker has organized the lecture in a cause/effect pattern are as follows:

causes	therefore	is a consequence of
leads to	due to	is caused by
results in / is the result of	because of	the effect is / is an effect of

See Part 2, Unit 4, pages 72–73 for more information on the cause and effect pattern.

A. *Read the following passage, which is part of an assigned reading for the lecture you will hear in this unit. Underline the main topic of the reading and any cause/effect signal words or phrases.*

> **Useful Terms**
>
> **distribute:** (noun: *distribution*) – to provide goods for sale, such as food, to stores and companies in a particular area
>
> > **Example**
> >
> > *The new sports drink is being* **distributed** *internationally by the Coca-Cola© Company.*
>
> **manufacture:** to use machines in a factory to make goods, usually in large numbers
>
> > **Example**
> >
> > *I work for a company that* **manufactures** *the best-selling brand of frozen pies.*
>
> **preserve:** to add something to food so that it will stay in good condition for a long time
>
> > **Example**
> >
> > *Fish can be* **preserved** *by rubbing it with salt and sugar and smoking it over a low fire.*
>
> **process:** to make food ready for sale, for example by preserving or changing it in some way
>
> > **Example**
> >
> > *Some foods are* **processed** *with chemicals to make them smell and taste better.*
>
> **standardize:** to make all the things of one particular type the same as each other
>
> > **Example**
> >
> > *The meat company* **standardized** *the size of its hamburgers so that any number of them would finish cooking at the same time.*

A History of Food Production in the United States

The history of food in the United States is directly connected to innovations in technology that happened nearly 300 years ago. However, in order to understand the important impact these new technologies had on what people ate, we need to look back at an even earlier time. During the seventeenth century, fresh vegetables and fruit could only be eaten during the season in which they grew. Also during that time, a majority of meat came from hunting deer, turkey, and other wild animals. The effect of living without the modern convenience of refrigerators or freezers was that most people had to rely on ancient methods of manually smoking, salting, and drying to preserve food. In those days, there was no fast shipping by trucks, trains, or planes to huge supermarkets where one could buy fresh foods from all over the world throughout the year. Because of the lack of high-speed transportation, people in that century had a limited diet; they generally ate only what was available locally or could be grown within a small area around where they lived.

However, machine-driven technologies introduced in the eighteenth and nineteenth centuries resulted in enormous changes in farming practices and in the way food was manufactured and delivered. By the beginning of the nineteenth century, people in the United States could buy more food than ever before. Because more farm products could be shipped by railroads to the growing population in cities, they were cheaper. Industry grew and refrigeration became more common, leading to an increase in the variety and quantity of fresh food available. By the late nineteenth century, food was produced in large amounts, standardized, and marketed to an ever-growing number of people. Factories with powerful machinery began to process, preserve, can, and package a large variety of foods. As a consequence, these processed foods were distributed throughout the country and became an increasingly important part of the nation's diet.

B. Use the information you underlined in Exercise A to complete the following notes. Use abbreviations and symbols and write down only the most important information.

Main Topic:

Cause	Effect
frsh veg & fruit - eat in season & meat ← hunt wild animal	
no refrig or freezer	
	lmted diet, ate food available locally
	change farm practice & way food manfctr & delivr
	begin 19th cent - people in US buy ++ food than b/4
++ farm product ship by RR to ↑ pop in cities	
industry ↑, refrig ↑	
	processed food distribute throughout & ↑ imprt prt nation's diet

C. To prepare to listen to the lecture, look up any new words from the reading in the dictionary.

LISTENING TASK

Before You Listen

A. Vocabulary Preview *Work with a partner. Review these vocabulary words from Units 1 through 4. Take turns explaining them in your own words. Use a dictionary if necessary.*

calorie	deadly	incredible	significantly
challenging	device	obvious	(adjective:
chemical	evidence	(adverb:	*significant*)
complex	impression	*obviously*)	trigger
		reaction	
		reinforce	

B. Predict *You will hear a lecture about fast food. Look at the speaker's notes on the board. What information do you think will be included in the lecture?*

> Fast food – soft drinks, hamburgers, French fries
>
> Drive-in & drive-through restaurants with microphones
>
> hamburger in NYC = hamburger in LA
>
> more calories than needed – unhealthy
>
> The Slow Food Movement

While You Listen

Remember

Keep in mind any note-taking skills that you felt needed to be improved after you evaluated your notes in Unit 5. These may include:

1. Choosing a format that works the best for the main topic of the lecture.
2. Writing the main ideas on the left and the details on the right.
3. Writing down key content words.
4. Not writing every word that you hear and omitting words that don't contribute important meaning.
5. Using symbols and abbreviations.
6. Listening for signal words and expressions that tell you what is important to include in your notes.

Food and Technology:
Is Faster Really Better?

A. 🎧 *Listen to a lecture about fast food. Take notes on a separate piece of paper. Remember to review and use the information that the speaker has written on the board.*

> **Tip**
> Listen for signal words and phrases that tell you the cause and the effect of an event.

B. *Work with a partner. Compare your notes from the lecture. Discuss any differences.*

Second Listening

🎧 **Check Your Notes** *Listen to the lecture again and check your notes. Add any information you missed or change any incorrect information. Then check your answers with your teacher.*

After You Listen

These exercises will help you evaluate how well you understand and can use the notes you took on the lecture about fast food.

■ EXERCISE 1

A. *Use your notes to answer the following questions.*

1. What is the main topic of this lecture?

   a. the history of fast-food restaurants and food producers in the United States

   b. how fast-food manufacturing technology was developed and how it is used today

   c. why the fast-food industry expanded and what effects it has had on diets in the United States

(continued)

2. According to the speaker, what is the specific definition of "fast food" that is currently in use?

   a. frozen, extremely processed, and standardized food

   b. inexpensive, quickly prepared fresh food

   c. cheaply manufactured, salt-preserved food

3. According to the lecture, which of the following are added during the processing and cooking of fast food? Check (✓) **two** items.

   ☐ fat   ☐ chemicals

   ☐ pepper   ☐ starch

4. Which of the following is **not** mentioned as an improvement in earlier technologies that caused the development of the fast-food industry?

   a. car and truck engines

   b. international distribution systems

   c. refrigeration technology

5. According to the speaker, why did fast-food drive-in restaurants become popular?

   a. They offered drivers quick service and an easy way to get food.

   b. They were located closer to people's homes than other restaurants.

   c. They appeared near convenient indoor parking areas.

6. What can be inferred about drive-through restaurants?

   a. People had to drive up to a window to order.

   b. People could phone in orders ahead from home.

   c. People had to wait in their cars for a long time

7. In this lecture, the speaker says that a fast-food restaurant could serve the exact same food in different cities. Do the sentences below describe causes of that effect? Check (✓) *Yes* or *No*.

	Yes	No
a. Food manufacturers could quickly ship food directly from farms to restaurants.		
b. Standardized food could be processed and kept cold in factories.		
c. Food delivered from centrally located factories could be sold for less money.		
d. Fast-food restaurants could standardize food for the needs of people in specific cities.		

8. The speaker probably mentions how trains and trucks were equipped because

   a. she wants to indicate that this method of shipping was fast.

   b. she is emphasizing the effects of technological innovations.

   c. she is using it as an example of how fast food is processed.

9. Which of the following are causes of people eating too much fast food? Check (✔) **two** sentences.

☐ The size of the food items is too large.

☐ The amount of calories is average.

☐ It has too much sugar in it.

☐ It is prepared too quickly.

10. What does the speaker say are the effects of eating too much fast food? Write your answers.

a. _____

b. _____

11. What can be inferred about why the Slow Food Movement was organized?

a. because it is opposed to fast food

b. because it wants to promote better fast food

c. because there are no other organized groups

12. Which of the following is **not** mentioned as an idea suggested by the Slow Food Movement?

a. eating foods in season

b. eating foods popular in the past

c. eating foods that are locally grown

13. What example does the speaker use to illustrate the positive effects of organizations like Slow Food?

a. The fast food industry is buying locally grown foods.

b. People are spending more time shopping and preparing food.

c. Governments are passing laws to deal with the fast-food industry.

14. How does the speaker feel about fast food?

a. She wants people to eat smaller amounts of it.

b. She thinks it should be processed in a better way.

c. She feels that it is unhealthy and should be avoided.

B. Compare your answers with a partner. Then check your answers with your teacher.

■ EXERCISE 2

Work with a partner. Review the incorrect answers in Exercise 1. Take turns explaining the reasons that the answers were incorrect. Use your notes to help you find the reasons.

Example
. . . .

> *For Number 1, answer (a) is incorrect because food producers aren't a main topic. Answer (b) is also incorrect because the focus of the lecture is not on food manufacturing technology.*

Listening for Pleasure

Unit Warm Up

Work with a partner. Read the joke aloud. Do you understand it? Why is it funny?

A: What's the longest word in the English language?

B: "Smiles." Because there's a mile between the first letter and the last one!

INTRODUCTION

Humor and Stand-Up Comedy

Why is humor so important? It's a fact that laughter makes us feel better. Laughter reduces stress and helps us relax. While it can be challenging to understand humor in a language other than our own, it is an essential part of learning to understand another language and culture.

In a stand-up comedy routine, a comedian performs on stage in front of a live audience. This "stand-up comic" makes the audience laugh by telling jokes or funny stories or acting silly. Stand-up comics usually create an act made up of a quick-paced series of short jokes and one-liners (jokes that are delivered in a single statement) or longer stories. Generally, the stand-up comic delivers a monologue, a story told by one person that reveals his or her amusing thoughts, speaking directly to the audience.

Stand-up comedy is popular worldwide. You can see a variety of live shows at comedy clubs—nightclubs or restaurants that offer stand-up comedy. Entire television networks have also developed original programs featuring stand-up comics. The Internet has further helped to promote stand-up comedy with various websites that offer millions of people the chance to view videos of stand-up comedians. People that love stand-up can now see a number of their favorite comedians almost anytime they choose.

Stand-up humor can involve three kinds of joke-telling techniques:

- a play on words or a pun — a word or phrase that has two different meanings or two words that sound nearly the same are used for a humorous effect

Example

> *Why is it that when you transport something by car, it's called a "shipment" but when you transport something by ship, it's called "cargo"?*

- an unexpected ending—a joke that presents a final statement or explanation that is a complete surprise

- a misunderstanding or confusion—a joke that involves a situation in which one person doesn't understand what is happening and this causes a humorous situation

A. *Work with a partner. Discuss these questions.*

1. Do you like to watch comedy shows on television? If so, what shows do you like? Why are they funny to you?

2. How often do you watch comedy movies? If you don't like comedies, explain why not. If you do, name your favorite comedy or one that you saw recently. Explain the story in the movie and why it was funny to you.

3. Have you ever been to a comedy club or seen a stand-up comedian on television? Did you enjoy the comedian's act? Why or why not?

4. Do you like telling jokes? Why or why not?

B. *Read these examples of jokes. Why is each joke funny? Choose from the following reasons. Write the letter next to the joke:*

a. a play on words

b. an unexpected ending

c. a misunderstanding or confusion

_____ 1. The man who worked at the watch factory was very funny. He spent his whole day making faces.

_____ 2. Two lions are eating a clown. One says to the other, "Does this taste funny to you?"

_____ 3. The evening news on television is where they begin with "Good evening" and then go on to tell you why it isn't.

_____ 4. Did you know that dolphins are so smart that within a few weeks after they are captured, they can train people to stand on the very edge of their pool and throw them fish?

_____ 5. *A woman takes her son to the doctor:*

Doctor: "What's wrong with your son?"
Mother: "He thinks he's a chicken."
Doctor: "Really? How long has he thought this?"
Mother: "Three years."
Doctor: "Three years!"
Mother: "Well, we would have brought him to see you sooner, but we needed the eggs."

_____ 6. One day a little girl came home from school and said to her mother, "Mommy, today in school the teacher got mad at me for something that I didn't do."

The mother was upset and said, "That's terrible! I'm going to have a talk with your teacher about this! By the way, what was it that you didn't do?"
The little girl replied, "My homework."

LISTENING TASK

You will hear a stand-up routine by a comedian named Lucky Jack. The kind of comedy that Lucky Jack uses in his routine is called "observational comedy." This style of humor involves making observations or comments about events or situations in everyday life. Lucky Jack makes some funny observations about airports and air travel.

> **Note**
> The jokes in observational comedy often begin with such introductory phrases as, "Have you ever noticed …?", "Now, think about it …," or "Here's the really funny thing …". Listen for these phrases in the comedy routine.

Stand-up comics usually tell short stories or describe specific situations. Pay attention to *where* the action in the story is taking place, *who* the people in the stories are, and *what* they and the comic are *saying* or *doing*.

Part 1

> **Useful Terms**
> **put your hands together:** an expression used to ask people in an audience to clap their hands or applaud
>
> **make it [somewhere] on time:** to arrive somewhere at the correct time
>
> **count on:** to depend on someone or something
>
> **flight path:** the route or course that an airplane takes
>
> **beverage cart:** a moveable tray with wheels from which different kinds of drinks (soda, juice, coffee) are served on an airplane
>
> **go bankrupt:** to be unable to pay your debts; to have no money
>
> **take [something] out on [someone]:** to direct (or misdirect) one's anger onto someone else
>
> **personnel:** workers or employees

A. 🎧 *Listen to Part 1 of the comedy routine.*

B. *Work with a partner. Discuss these questions.*

1. What are some of the events or problems that always make Lucky Jack late when he flies? Have you ever had problems like these when you have traveled? Have you had other problems when you travel that made you late? Explain.

2. Lucky Jack describes the airport as "Airportland," a place with "its own laws and economy." What are the things he complains about in Airportland? Do you agree?

Part 2

> **Useful Terms**
>
> **armrest:** an attached part of a seat designed to support the arm of a person sitting in it
>
> **interference:** an unwanted noise or electronic source that causes a problem with electrical equipment
>
> **cruise:** to travel at a steady speed in an airplane, car, or boat
>
> **munch:** to eat something in a noisy way
>
> **mini-pretzel:** a small version of a salty type of snack
>
> **health insurance:** an arrangement with a company in which you pay money regularly and the company pays the costs of medical care if you are hurt or sick
>
> **commuter flight:** short airplane flight that people take regularly to get to work
>
> **seat cushion:** a bag filled with soft material, used to make a seat more comfortable
>
> **flotation device:** an object used to help you stay above the surface of water without sinking
>
> **desert:** an area of land where it is usually hot and dry, with few plants and often a lot of sand

A. 🎧 *Listen to Part 2 of the comedy routine.*

B. *Work with a partner. Discuss these questions.*

1. What does Lucky Jack say is the problem with the armrests on the airplane seats? Have you ever noticed this before?

2. The flight attendant told Lucky Jack to turn off his iPod. Do you listen to music on an electronic device or use a laptop computer when you fly? Have you ever forgotten to turn it off and had the flight attendant tell you to do so? If so, how did this make you feel?

3. What is happening to the woman in row 14? Who helps her? What idea does this give Lucky Jack?

4. Because of the situation with the woman in row 14, what happens to Lucky Jack's flight?

5. Why does the safety announcement, "In the unlikely event of a water landing, your seat cushions can be used as flotation devices" annoy Lucky Jack? Do you listen carefully to the safety announcements every time you fly? Why or why not?

Part 3

A. *Work in groups of three. Before you listen to Part 3, have each person choose one of these situations to listen to. After you listen, you will be asked to retell the situation you chose.*

- The description of Lucky Jack's luggage and luggage tag and what happens to them
- Where he goes after the situation with his luggage and luggage tag, how he acts, and what the airline gives him
- What happens in the hotel room that almost makes him late for his performance

B. 🎧 *Listen to Part 3 of the comedy routine. Here are some clues to listen for:*

- Why is Lucky Jack's luggage tag unusual?
- What does he say about the people in the office where he goes? What do these people do for him? Why?
- What does the sign on the third door in his hotel room say?
- What does Lucky Jack do with the sign and why? What happens afterward?

C. *Work with your group. Take turns retelling the situations you chose in Exercise A.*

After You Listen

■ EXERCISE 1

Another popular kind of joke is called a "knock-knock" joke. The first person pretends he or she is knocking on the door. These jokes always follow the same form and play with words that sound alike.

A. Work with a partner. Read these knock-knock jokes aloud.

1.

A: *Knock, Knock*

B: *Who's there?*

A: *Lettuce!*

B: *Lettuce who?*

A: *Lettuce in and I'll tell you!*

2.

A: *Knock, Knock*

B: *Who's there?*

A: *Apple!*

B: *Apple who?*

A: *Apple your hair if you don't let me in!*

3.

A: *Knock, Knock*

B: *Who's there?*

A: *Norway!*

B: *Norway who?*

A: *Norway will I leave until you open this door!*

B. Talk with your partner. What is the play on words in each knock-knock joke? Write the real meanings of these words.

1. Lettuce = _____

2. Apple = _____

3. Norway = _____

■ EXERCISE 2

A. Read the incomplete jokes. Then, look at the punch lines (surprise endings) that follow. Write the letter of the correct punch line after each joke. There are three extra punch lines.

1. A young doctor was just setting up his first office when his secretary told him a man was there to see him. The doctor wanted to make a good first impression by having the man think he was successful and very busy. He told his secretary to bring the man into his office.

    As soon as the man entered his office, the doctor picked up the telephone and pretended to be having a conversation with a patient. The man waited until the "conversation" was over. Then the doctor put the telephone down and asked, "Can I help you?"

    To which the man replied,

    _____ Punch line

2. A young man was hired by a supermarket and reported for his first day of work. The manager greeted him with a warm handshake and a smile, gave him a broom, and said, "Your first job will be to sweep out the store."

    The young man was annoyed and replied, "But I'm a college graduate."

    "Oh, I'm sorry. I didn't know that," said the manager,

    _____ Punch line

(continued)

3. Two friends were having a conversation after work at a restaurant.

One said, "You don't look very happy. What's up?"

"I just found out that I talk in my sleep."

"Well, that's not such a big problem."

_____ Punch line

Punch lines:

a. "Here, give me the broom . . . I'll show you how."

b. "Yes, I'd like to know who you were talking to just now."

c. "I wish I knew what I said."

d. "No, I'm just here to connect your telephone."

e. "It is when it disturbs the other workers in the office."

f. "What did you study?"

B. *Work in a group. Have each group member choose one of the jokes from Exercise A. Practice telling your jokes in pairs. Then take turns telling the joke to the group without reading it. You can use your own words.*

■ EXERCISE 3

Think of something funny that happened to you when you were traveling. Make notes about where you were and what happened. Then tell your own funny travel story to your classmates.

A Radio Play—The *Crimson Parrot:* The Glory of the Seas

Unit Warm Up

A. *Read the passage about the Golden Age of Radio.*

In the 1930s and 40s, the radio was a very important source of family entertainment in many homes.

The Golden Age of Radio

Can you imagine life before television? Well, way back in the early to mid 20th century, there was just such a time when families gathered with excitement around the radios in their living rooms to listen to a wide variety of shows. Radio was the newest and most popular entertainment technology at the time. It reached its high point during the 1930s and 1940s, now known as the Golden Age of Radio.

During the Golden Age of Radio, there were thousands of programs that appealed to everyone from children to adults. They included live music, comedies, mysteries, science fiction and detective stories, and adventures on the wide-open seas. The dramatic series featured realistic sound effects, such as the sound of footsteps, doors being opened and closed, rain, fire . . . You name it, and Foley sound effects artists could produce it. (See Part 3, Unit 2, for more information on Foley artists and sound effects.) Weekly episodes—or parts—of radio dramas captured the imaginations of people all over the world with their well-written stories, colorfully detailed settings, and appealing characters.

B. Work with a partner. Discuss these questions.

1. How do you think listening to a radio drama in the 1940s was different from watching television now? What do you think the advantages (or disadvantages) of both radio and television are?

2. It has been said that listening to radio during the Golden Age of Radio brought families closer together. Why do you think this might have been true? Do you think it is also true today for television?

3. Would you enjoy listening to a radio drama? Why or why not?

4. If you think you would enjoy a radio drama, what kind would you like to listen to the most? For example, would you like to listen to a mystery, a science fiction story, or a detective story?

INTRODUCTION

Get ready to listen to a radio play written in the style of those from the Golden Age of Radio. You will also hear a commercial for breakfast cereal. It was common for radio plays to be partially paid for by a company, which in return was allowed to advertise its products during the play. Typical of popular dramas of that time, this play presents an adventure of the crew of a ship called the *Crimson Parrot*. The *Crimson Parrot* takes its name from a dark red (crimson) tropical bird (a parrot). The ship has sailed to a far-away island, Malengi, where the people aboard the Crimson Parrot meet some very interesting characters.

A. Read the cast of characters for the radio show you will hear in this unit. Note each character's occupation.

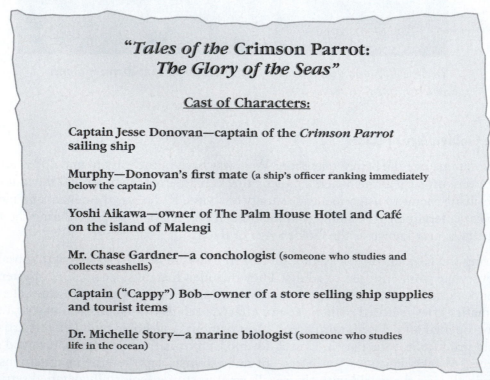

**"Tales of the Crimson Parrot:
The Glory of the Seas"**

<u>Cast of Characters:</u>

**Captain Jesse Donovan—captain of the *Crimson Parrot*
sailing ship**

Murphy—Donovan's first mate (a ship's officer ranking immediately below the captain)

**Yoshi Aikawa—owner of The Palm House Hotel and Café
on the island of Malengi**

Mr. Chase Gardner—a conchologist (someone who studies and collects seashells)

**Captain ("Cappy") Bob—owner of a store selling ship supplies
and tourist items**

Dr. Michelle Story—a marine biologist (someone who studies life in the ocean)

B. *Before you take off on the adventure with Captain Donovan, look the picture of the Crimson Parrot ship. Write the vocabulary words from the picture next to the correct definitions below.*

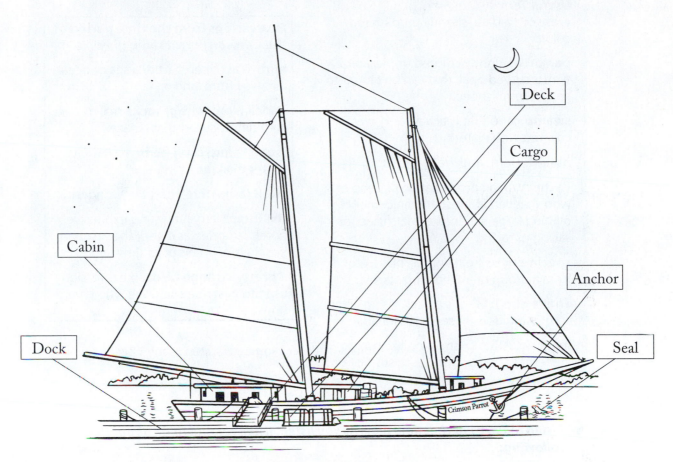

_____ **1.** a room on a ship used for sleeping

_____ **2.** goods that are carried in a ship, airplane, or truck

_____ **3.** the flat top part of a ship that you can walk on

_____ **4.** a place where goods are put into or taken off of ships; usually built near or on the water

_____ **5.** a large sea animal with smooth fur

_____ **6.** the heavy piece of metal that is dropped into the water to stop a ship from moving

LISTENING TASK

You will hear the radio play in five parts. Each part begins with Captain Donovan reading an entry from the *ship's log*, a record of daily events like a diary or journal, written by the captain of a sailing ship. You will discuss questions after each part.

Part 1

Useful Terms

crimson: a dark, slightly purplish red color

parrot: a brightly colored tropical bird with a curved beak that can be taught to copy human speech

swamp: land that is always very wet or covered with water

humid: warm and wet weather

yacht club: an organization of people who share an interest and enjoyment in owning large expensive boats used for sailing or racing

specimen: a single animal, plant, etc. from a group of animals, plants, etc.

That's nuts!: "That's crazy!" – said when something doesn't seem reasonable

fishy: 1. tasting or smelling like fish
2. seeming bad or dishonest; suspicious

Expressions from the time period of the *Crimson Parrot* radio play:

high seas: open part of a sea or ocean far away from land

knock [someone's] socks off: to completely surprise or amaze

[something] can't be beat: to be better than [anything else]

swell (adjective): great or wonderful

the Ritz: a very fancy and expensive hotel; regarded as one of the first and best luxury hotels of its time

a pretty strange bird: an expression used to describe someone who is very unusual

---

A. 🎧 *Listen to Part 1 of the radio play. As you listen, listen for and think about the following:*

- **The characters:** Based on the tone of the character's voice and the style of speech or dress, what kind of personalities does each one have? What do you imagine they look like?

- **The scene:** What kind of place is the island? What kind of place is Yoshi Aikawa's hotel and café?

- **The story:** What is happening? Why is each character on the island of Malengi? How do the characters interact with each other? What are they doing or going to do?

- **Sound effects (SFX):** How do the sound effects help paint a picture in your mind of the characters, the place, and the action?

- **Clues:** Like all good, old-time radio dramas, a mystery forms around the characters, so listen for the clues that will help you understand the story and predict what will happen next.

  Relax and have fun!

B. Work with a partner. Discuss these questions.

1. According to Captain Donovan's description, what kind of place is the island of Malengi?

2. What's your impression of Captain Donovan? What kind of character is the Captain's first mate, Murphy?

3. What kind of person do you think Mr. Chase Gardner is based on his clothing, attitude, and speech? What has he been doing in Malengi? Why does Yoshi Aikawa introduce him to Donovan and Murphy?

4. What are Captain Donovan and Murphy's attitudes toward Mr. Gardner? Why do they have this opinion?

5. Think about what Cappy Bob, the owner of the store selling ship supplies and tourist items says about seashells: "There are some pretty rare specimens around here." Based on this clue, predict what will happen next.

Part 2

Get ready to meet another important character, Dr. Michelle Story. Listen for how the other characters react to her.

> **Useful Terms**
> **cast off:** to untie the rope that keeps a boat near shore so that it can sail away
>
> **jade:** a stone, ranging in color from deep green, yellow and brown to white; commonly used for jewelry
>
> **made-up:** not real; false or fake
>
> **marine:** 1. (adjective) referring to the ocean and the animals and plants that live there 2. (noun) a soldier who often serves on a ship
>
> **Expressions from the time period of the *Crimson Parrot* radio play:**
>
> **..., see?:** used as a question word at the end of a sentence to mean "Do you understand?"; (considered impolite and aggressive)
>
> **dame:** a woman (not generally in current use; informal)

A. 🎧 **Listen to Part 2 of the radio play.**

B. Work with a partner. Discuss these questions.

1. Captain Donovan responds to Mr. Gardner's request to hurry to get to Tahiti by saying, "Look, Gardner, the *Crimson Parrot*'s not your private yacht. It's a trading ship, and it's *my* ship, see? I give the orders here." What does this tell you about Donovan's personality?

2. What is Donovan's reaction to Dr. Michelle Story?

3. How does Mr. Gardner feel about Dr. Story? Why does he feel this way?

4. Based on what Mr. Gardner says about Dr. Story ("That so-called doctor can't be trusted … Trouble is what she is"), predict what you think will happen next aboard the *Crimson Parrot*.

Part 3

Useful Terms

brisk: strong and fast

carving: an object that has been cut from wood, stone, etc.

buck: one dollar (informal)

Expressions from the time period of the *Crimson Parrot* radio play:

toots: a way of addressing a woman (not commonly in current use; informal)

brig: a place on a ship used to temporarily lock up criminals; a ship's jail

doozie: something extraordinary and wonderful

A. *Work in groups of three. Before you listen to Part 3, have each person choose one of the following characters to listen to. After you listen, you will retell the story from that character's point of view.*

- **Captain Donovan**
- **Mr. Gardner**
- **Dr. Michelle Story**

B. 🎧 *Listen to Part 3 of the radio play. Hopefully by now you've gotten to know the characters better. Here are some clues to listen for:*

- What happens in Mr. Gardner's cabin?
- How does Mr. Gardner react? Donovan? Dr. Story?
- After the event, what happens to Dr. Story?
- What does Mr. Gardner show Donovan? Why is it important?

C. *Work with your group. Take turns retelling the story. Play the role of the character you chose in Exercise A. Follow these instructions:*

- **Dr. Michelle Story:** Explain what you were doing in Mr. Gardner's cabin. What happened after? How do you feel about it?
- **Mr. Gardner:** Explain why you think Dr. Story was in your cabin. How do you feel about it? What do you want Donovan to do about it? Give details about your Glory of the Seas. What do you think Dr. Story might do?
- **Captain Donovan:** Explain what happened in Mr. Gardner's cabin. How did you react? What is your impression of the Glory of the Seas?

Part 4A

This part of the radio show is going to be exciting! You'll have to listen carefully to what Dr. Story has to say about two kinds of seashells, the Glory of the Seas and the Queen of the Seas.

> **Useful Terms**
>
> **mist:** clouds that are close to the ground or water's surface, making it difficult to see very far; fog
>
> **bump:** an injury that causes the skin to swell up because you have hit it on something or been hit by something
>
> **gag:** a piece of cloth tied over someone's mouth so he or she cannot make any noise
>
> **nod:** to move one's head up and down, especially to show agreement or understanding
>
> **breathtaking:** amazing; incredible
>
> **switch:** to replace one object with another similar object secretly or accidentally
>
> **nasty:** serious or painful-looking
>
> **Aussie:** a shortened form used to refer to people from Australia (i.e., Australians)
>
> **Expressions from the time period of the _Crimson Parrot_ radio play:**
>
> **moxie:** courage combined with cleverness

A. 🎧 **Listen to Part 4A of the radio play.**

B. You heard those sound effects, right? Based on what you heard, predict what you think just happened. Tell the class your ideas.

Part 4B

OK, now let's get back to the radio play to see what did happen.

🎧 **Listen to Part 4B of the radio play. Then work with a partner. Discuss these questions.**

1. What happened to Captain Donovan? Give details about where he is and how he is feeling.
2. What is the difference between the Queen of the Seas seashell and the Glory of the Seas seashell?
3. What did Dr. Story actually do when she was in Mr. Gardner's cabin?
4. What is Dr. Story's attitude toward Mr. Gardner?
5. Where did she get the seashells?
6. What does Dr. Story _say_ she is going to do with the seashell?
7. What does Dr. Story do at the end of Part 4?
8. What is Captain Donovan's reaction to what Dr. Story does?

Part 5

Did you figure out what happened to Mr. Gardner's Glory of the Seas? If not, listen carefully to the end of the story.

> *Useful Terms*
> **pirate's chest:** a large container with an attached lid used by pirates to store stolen goods
>
> **grand (noun):** a thousand dollars (informal)
>
> **ground:** 1. (past tense verb of *grind*) to crush or break up into tiny pieces or powder 2. (noun) the surface of the earth under your feet when you are outside; soil or dirt
>
> **Expressions from the time period of the *Crimson Parrot* radio play:**
>
> **cuppa joe:** cup of coffee (not in current use)

A. 🎧 *Listen to Part 5 of the radio play. Here are some clues to listen for in order to help you understand the surprise ending:*

- Who did Cappy Bob sell the Glory of the Seas to? the Queen of the Seas? How many of each did he sell to each person?

- How many of the Glory of the Seas does Cappy Bob have? Why is this important?

- Why doesn't Cappy Bob sell more than one of the Glory of the Seas to each person?

B. *Work with a partner. Discuss these questions.*

1. Who did Cappy Bob sell the Glory of the Seas to? Who did he sell the Queen of the Seas to?

2. What is the difference between a Glory of the Seas and a Queen of the Seas seashell? Why is that important to the story? What does it mean for Mr. Gardner?

3. How many Glory of the Seas did Dr. Story swim away with? Why does she want them and what will she likely do with them?

4. How many Glory of the Seas does Cappy Bob have? Why doesn't he sell them for more money?

5. Based on what Cappy Bob says about the future value of the Glory of the Seas, do you think Dr. Story will get the results she hoped for in the end? Why or why not?

6. Did you predict the surprise ending—that Dr. Story took Mr. Gardner's valuable Glory of the Seas seashell out of his briefcase and replaced it with a less valuable seashell?

After You Listen

■ EXERCISE 1

You probably figured out that Dr. Story took Mr. Gardner's valuable Glory of the Seas seashell out of his briefcase and replaced it with a less valuable seashell, the Queen of the Seas. Now, just for fun, work in groups, discuss and imagine the pasts and futures of the characters in "The Glory of the Seas" episode from the *Crimson Parrot* radio play:

1. How do you think Murphy became Captain Donovan's first mate? Use your imagination to create a past story for him and how he met Captain Donovan.

2. How do you think Cappy Bob got to the island of Malengi? What about Yoshi Aikawa? Why do they stay there? Create some mysterious past that led them to the island and secrets that keep them there.

3. What will happen to the wealthy Mr. Chase Gardner when he returns to San Francisco? Imagine that he has a powerful and rich family and how they will react to his failed effort to bring home a valuable Glory of the Seas.

4. Who is Dr. Michelle Story? Is she really a scientist? Does she have a dark past? What do you think she will do when she discovers her Glory of the Seas isn't as valuable as she thought?

5. Finally, dream up a new adventure for Captain Donovan. Where will he sail the *Crimson Parrot* next? What will he find there?

■ EXERCISE 2

It was common in radio dramas like "Tales of the *Crimson Parrot*" to use humorous and creative comparisons to create powerful images in the minds of the listeners.

Example

> *Captain Donovan says when he walks into the Palm House Hotel and Café, "It takes a few minutes for my eyes to get used to the darkness—it's like a coal mine inside, even in mid-afternoon."*
>
> *A coal mine, a hole dug deep underground to remove coal, is a very dark place. The captain is comparing the hotel and café to a coal mine to show just how dark the hotel and café is.*

Now, it's your turn to come up with some colorful comparisons and expressions. Read the expressions from the "The Glory of the Seas" episode and then, working with a partner, take turns creating your own expressions to describe each topic.

1. Topic: the weather

   Captain Donovan: "It's … humid enough to drown a butterfly."

   Describe very hot or very cold weather:

   It's _____ enough to _____ .

Example

> *It's hot enough to fry eggs on the sidewalk.*

(continued)

2. Topic: the color of someone's hair and eyes

   Captain Donovan: "She [Dr. Michelle Story] has long hair the color of autumn leaves and eyes the color of green jade."

   Describe the color of someone's hair and eyes:

   She or he has hair the color of _____ and eyes the color of
   _____.

3. Topic: someone who is frightened or surprised

   Captain Donovan: "… and there's the doctor [Dr. Michelle Story], her face as red as the carving of the crimson parrot back in her cabin."

   Describe someone whose face looks frightened or surprised:

   His/her face was as _____ (color) as _____.

4. Topic: a physical injury

   Captain Donovan: "I probably have a bump on my head the size of a duck egg."

   Describe a physical injury like a bump, cut, or bruise:

   I have a _____ on my _____ the size/color
   of a _____.

5. Topic: how someone does a physical activity

   Captain Donovan: "She [Dr. Michelle Story] swims, well, like a seal. Like a red-haired seal."

   Describe how someone does a physical activity like swimming, running, skiing, jumping:

   He/she _____ like a _____.

6. Topic: how something tastes

   Captain Donovan: "You know Yoshi's coffee tastes like mud."

   Describe how something tastes, good or bad:

   _____ tastes like _____.

■ **EXERCISE 3**

Work with a partner. Create a short role play using some of the expressions you wrote in Exercise 2. You can include the weather in a place where your character(s) are and describe how the character(s) look, feel, do an activity, using the expressions you created. When you are finished, take turns reading your role play aloud.

Further Listening If you would like to listen to more radio shows from the Golden Age of Radio, you can find many available on the Internet. To search for these radio shows, use the key words old-time radio show or classic radio.

Credits